IN GOD'S PRESENCE

Worship in the Bible

The nature of music

Music's role in worship

■

COART RAMEY

BIBLE
MODULAR
SERIES

Bob Jones University Press, Greenville, South Carolina 29614

This textbook was written by members of the faculty and staff of Bob Jones University. Standing for the "old-time religion" and the absolute authority of the Bible since 1927, Bob Jones University is the world's leading Fundamentalist Christian university. The staff of the University is devoted to educating Christian men and women to be servants of Jesus Christ in all walks of life.

Providing unparalleled academic excellence, Bob Jones University prepares its students through its offering of over one hundred majors, while its fervent spiritual emphasis prepares their minds and hearts for service and devotion to the Lord Jesus Christ.

If you would like more information about the spiritual and academic opportunities available at Bob Jones University, please call
1-800-BJ-AND-ME (1-800-252-6363).
www.bju.edu

NOTE:
The fact that materials produced by other publishers may be referred to in this volume does not constitute an endorsement by Bob Jones University Press of the content or theological position of materials produced by such publishers. The position of Bob Jones University Press, and the University itself, is well known. Any references and ancillary materials are listed as an aid to the student or the teacher and in an attempt to maintain the accepted academic standards of the publishing industry.

In God's Presence

Coart Ramey, M.A.

ISBN 1-57924-377-0

15 14 13 12 11 10 9 8 7 6 5 4 3 2 1

CONTENTS

Introduction

God's people have faced the same problems throughout all ages. Although the events of the Bible can seem very distant, characters in the Bible were essentially like modern Christians. They lived in a different world in many ways, but their human nature was the same. Their relationships with God and with each other and their struggles to live for Him are familiar to anyone who can see through the barriers of time, language, and culture.

This book develops its message through a fictional story. But fiction, whether ancient or modern, hardly ever exists purely for entertainment. Stories teach something. One of the greatest skills education can provide is the ability to recognize when an author is trying to persuade you of something without your realizing it. As you read this story, think about what the author wants you to decide and believe.

When a subject is sensitive, it is best to approach it indirectly. For example, if you have two friends who are angry at each other, and you approach one of them to try to make him see that he is the individual at fault, you will probably start the conversation with something totally unrelated. When you do get to the problem, you are wise to bring it up in some way that is not offensive. Asking, "Is there something wrong between you and _____?" is better than declaring, "You were such a jerk to do that to _____!" The latter approach will only make your friend defensive, worsening the situation.

Josiah, the main character in the story you are about to read, faces a complex problem. By setting Josiah's story during the reign of King Solomon, the author seeks to help you see *principles* that underlie Josiah's struggle—a struggle that plagues Christians today. Josiah's story will give insights into a controversial issue without being unnecessarily offensive. No one is trying to trick you; this story carries a message that applies to everyone. Be open to expanding your own views and considering whether or not the Lord would have you change your thoughts and habits in some way.

On the surface, Josiah has to deal with problems about music. The real issue is somewhat deeper—but you can discover the underlying problem as you read. You can also consider how the Bible applies to Josiah's situation. Scripture provides an answer to every question a Christian will face. However, many questions can be answered only with an in-depth knowledge of the Bible and a thoughtful consideration of all the factors involved. Many practical issues have to be settled by broader scriptural principles that may not at first seem to apply.

Every situation is clear to God; humans are the ones who complicate matters by being diverse, confusing, confused, and downright sinful. Be assured that God does have a specific solution to every problem. Although finding out what God desires can take hard work and patience, the reward is well worth the trouble.

Solving Josiah's dilemma will require plenty of background knowledge. Hopefully, you will find this story from Josiah's life easy to read and remember. However, it is most important that you understand the issues involved in Josiah's problem and how they apply to you who, unlike Josiah, are real.

CHAPTER ONE

The Gift of a Levite

Josiah tightened the belt of his robe and gathered his things as his mind wandered away from the routine. He imagined leaping over the day to the evening; at the end of the day, he and Casil would practice slinging with the other guys. He also thought of eating supper as the sun went down, then stretching out on the roof to relax and watching the lamps appear. They would sparkle all over the city as families settled in for the evening, then vanish as the stars came out and people slept.

A call from downstairs struck Josiah out of his reverie. "Hurry, young man. The sun is about to rise!" *I know that, Mom,* Josiah thought. He shouldered his satchel and walked down to the front room. He took the breakfast loaf she offered and traded cheek kisses with her, then headed out the door.

He didn't think of his mother again for some time. He had to be at the palace of Jehovah by dawn for the morning offerings. Having been late twice in as many weeks, Josiah was taxing his supply of excuses. He bit off chunks of the tough little barley loaf and swallowed them dry as he trotted past the homes of his cousins and friends up toward the stone wall enclosing the grounds of the palaces.

Great cube-shaped stones rose in rows before him. He passed through an open square gateway, nodded to the guard, and entered the paved rectangular courtyard separating the northern wall of Jehovah's palace from the oblong building used by the Levites as a headquarters, storehouse, school, and meeting place. Josiah hurried up an exterior staircase onto the roof of the Levite building and winced when he saw the dawn sun over the city wall eastward.

Prayers had already started. One Levite teacher, standing to one side to observe such violations, gave Josiah a look promising that his tardiness was noted. Though the students in the back of the group were mostly older than he was, Josiah sat down among

Hittites

To Greece

Cyprus

The Great Sea

Aram

C a n a a n

Philistia

Ammon

Israel

Moab

Edom

EGYPT

The
Ancient
Near East

The
Great
Desert

The
Red Sea

them and tried to listen to the teachers as they led in prayer. These prayers always seemed interminable; Josiah felt more like going back to sleep.

One teacher began singing a familiar psalm with great feeling:

> Sons of man, until when will my glory be shame?
> Will you love worthlessness and seek deception?
> But know that Jehovah has set apart the faithful to Himself;
> Jehovah will hear when I call unto Him.

Josiah thought he was being too dramatic. The singer continued:

> Tremble, and do not sin.
> Converse with your hearts upon your beds, and be still.
> Sacrifice sacrifices of righteousness
> And trust in Jehovah.

Now that sounded good to Josiah. He'd love to be conversing with his heart on his bed right now!

After prayer, everyone stood and a bustle of conversation began. Josiah worked his way forward to join his own class. They were mostly yawning, stretching, and laughing at each other. "Oh-ooooo-WAH!" sang out a familiar baritone. "Get on key or stitch your mouth," Josiah ordered. "Ugly guys shouldn't draw attention to themselves, anyway." He grinned at Casil, who was not ugly and had not been off key despite his drowsiness.

"I just woke up," Casil replied, smiling.

Josiah looked down onto the inner court of Jehovah's palace, wondering if his father was nearby. His dad left home early each morning to help ready animals for the sacrifices. It was the kind of job Josiah had always thought was among the worst possible.

He looked at the bronze altar, rising on its platform in front of the palace itself. Sunlight gleamed gloriously off the two mighty bronze pillars and the door to the palace. The court was filled with white-robed priests carrying instruments or leading lambs.

A minute later a peal of trumpets announced the beginning of morning sacrifices. Everyone quieted and looked toward the altar.

The trumpets resumed on a lower note and began building toward a climax.

"Uh-oh, a rebel," muttered Casil. "Run, run!" he whispered loudly, drawing some snickers from the other boys. The rebel was one lamb destined for the morning sacrifice. Normally they were passive as the priests tied them and killed them, but something had startled this one. It nearly jumped off the altar before a struggling priest managed to restrain and calm it. Placidly, it allowed itself to be bound. The knife flashed as the officiating priest made a practiced cut, punctuated with Casil's grunting and gurgling impersonation of a dying animal. Josiah's vivid imagination recalled the last time he had watched his father offer a burnt offering for their family; the lamb hadn't made any noise, but the color and smell of its blood was enough to make Josiah queasy, even in memory.

After several animals were killed and their bodies properly divided, a priest set fire to the kindling piled on top of the altar. Flames sprang up and spread to each carcass. A smoky orange inferno glowed in the morning sun as the trumpet choir reached a climax. Josiah caught a slight smell of burnt flesh as their school choir leader stood in front of them and raised his arms. When he signaled, all the boys sang together,

> I will extol you, my God, O king!
> I will bless your name forever and ever.
> I will bless you every day,
> I will praise your name forever and ever.

On they sang through David's praise psalm. As he carried the tenor line, Josiah stared at the closed door to Jehovah's palace and wondered if He were pleased with the morning's slaughtered lambs.

Later that morning Josiah sat daydreaming while Master Johanon lectured his class about something concerned with David's psalms. Twenty boys were settled comfortably on the floor. Most were looking at Johanon perched on his bench up front, but a few looked at the walls, at the sky through the little windows, or at nothing in particular. Josiah was one of the latter. Suddenly, his reverie was again broken.

"Josiah. Josiah Ben-Adaiah." Hearing his name made him rack his memory for Johanon's last few sentences, but all he could remember was . . .

"Are you hearing me, young man?"

"I am, Master Johanon."

"Then why are you still sitting?"

Uh-oh. Josiah got to his feet quickly, desperately weighing his options for a course of action. But the class only exploded in laughter, startling him again and giving him a very self-conscious feeling.

Johanon merely closed his eyes as the burst of merriment passed and then said calmly, "I had not told you to stand up, Josiah. I asked whether Jehovah sees all men as sinners or sees them divided between sinners and those who are His people." Josiah remembered they were discussing the psalm called "The fool has said." Josiah had memorized the psalm years ago, of course, so he began to run through it in his mind as he sank back to the floor. There was the part about the fool denying God's presence, then Jehovah looks down on the children of men . . .

"No!" he said decisively. "I mean yes," he continued, "Jehovah sees all men as sinners, but no, he doesn't divide . . ." *Wait,* Josiah interrupted himself. *At one point it talks about Jehovah's people being devoured.*

"Does not Jehovah speak later of his people whom the wicked ones devour?" Johanon asked.

"Yes, sir."

"So Jehovah distinguishes sinners from His people?" asked Johanon.

Josiah knew he was looking bad, and searched his mind for what the teacher might want. "Yes, Israel is His people."

"Then does Jehovah see all men as sinners?"

"Man sinned in eating the forbidden fruit," agreed Josiah, resorting to safe ground.

"But in this psalm," prodded the teacher, "does Jehovah say so?"

Josiah's memory momentarily spun unfocused, then returned to the fifth line of the psalm. "The whole have turned aside, together they have become corrupt," he quoted.

"Exactly. Even though Jehovah has distinguished Israel from all other nations, still He calls us sinners with the rest of the sons of men. Yet the sinners He will punish are those who devour His people, as He says, 'Have all the workers of iniquity no knowledge? Who eat up my people as they eat bread?'"

Josiah was relieved to no longer be the center of attention. He half-listened to the routine lesson, looking forward more to the next part of the morning, when they would practice music.

Having finished his lesson on the words of the psalms, Johanon summoned the attention of his class. "Today your interpretation assignment is due. What did you do with 'The heavens declare'? Ready your instrument and give your mind to it for a little. I'll call on the first student shortly."

Josiah tried to concentrate on the words of the psalm and the tune he had composed, but his mind kept wandering. He thought of fighting in the king's army in a battle against the Arameans. There was some sighing and mumbling around the room as his classmates thought through their assigned text and their own new tunes. They had been given all week to write a musical score, but several had waited until the previous evening to compose something.

The problem with a composition assignment was that the range of familiar tunes to a famous psalm played through your head every time you tried to think up a new tune. Johanon would scoff if you followed an existing tune too closely but be annoyed if you deviated too far from what he considered acceptable.

"Zachariah," called Johanon. The boy by that name rose slowly and walked to the front carrying his lyre. He settled on the performer's bench and played a few introductory chords. Pausing, he adjusted his hold on the lyre. After preparing himself with a deep breath, he launched into his composition.

Most hymnists gave a "muttering" counter-melody to the first six verses of "The Heavens Declare" to represent the "noisy" creation telling about God. Zachariah tried nothing so difficult. He played a simple melody as he sang.

> The heavens are telling the glory of God,
> And the work of his hands the expanse is reporting.

The little song went on through a section about the running of the sun and into the law verses without any change in style. When he reached the confession of sin, Zachariah added some tension and raised his voice, then quickly let the song flow into a sweet resolution with the final petitions.

"Well done," judged Johanon. Josiah thought the song had been too shallow. But Johanon was a gracious teacher. "Baruk, next please."

Baruk's tune was poorly crafted, but he made a clever transition into the praises and petitions at the tenth verse. The next student made a distinct transition at verse seven from a joyous to a tranquil mood, but never really brought the music to a climax.

After three more students came Beriah's turn. He held his long lute at an angle and plucked a basic melody as he bellowed the words. Beriah had a powerful voice but a shortage of imagination. Josiah almost laughed as he listened to the boy charge through each line with no change in expression.

Jedan drew the thirteenth turn. He skillfully played on his harp a lilting tune that softened to become more meditative at verse seven and swelled to a climax before the end. *The best so far,* thought Josiah. The next five offerings were sound, but unremarkable.

"Let us stay awake, men," Johanon encouraged his drowsy class. "Casil." Casil rose with his great wooden pipe and sat confidently on the bench. He played a practice scale that ended with the sourest note Josiah had heard in weeks.

"Sorry," grinned Casil. "I'm a little short on practice today." He took a breath and began a rousing tune that woke up everyone. He soared up the scale and into a dance when he came to the verses about the sun bursting out of his chamber and running his race. At verse seven Casil dropped into a lively rendition of the next three verses, carried his song to a warm climax in the praise and petition section, then finished with a flourish.

Casil looked down as he walked back to his place beside Josiah. The class murmured approvingly. Josiah looked at Johanon. The old man's face was even, and he only said, "That showed a lot of hard work. Now, Josiah, finish for us, please."

"That was excellent," whispered Josiah to Casil as the latter sat. Casil was smiling, knowing he had done well. Josiah walked to the front.

Josiah braced his harp against his arm and body. He began the most powerful melody anyone had played all day. He wove a counter-melody around the main melody to personify the living, singing creation. Reaching the section about the sun, Josiah played rhythmically and triumphantly.

He made a sharp break before the beginning of the law stanza. His serene, dignified melody retained the basic harmony of the psalm's opening. The song flowed gently into the praise and petition section, built dissonance to convey the psalmist's struggle with sin, and blossomed perfectly into the climax and resolution.

The class was quiet. A few grunted or shook their heads in familiar amazement. "Very well done," Johanon stated flatly. "Good use of all the elements, and an effective conveyance of the psalm. You may take your place." Josiah rose and returned to sit by Casil.

Lunch was a relief from concentrating and a welcome reinforcement to Josiah's lone barley loaf. Josiah sat with Casil, Jedan, and Beriah under a sycamore tree in the garden of the Levite school. A few hundred boys ranging in age from ten to twenty sat around the landscaped garden. Many others had walked home for lunch and a nap, as Josiah often did. But today Casil had wanted to talk about something he called a "secret." Josiah looked at his friend and wondered what it would be this time. Casil always had an idea for an adventure or some bit of mischief. Josiah loved watching him plan something and then try to pull it off.

"He's a merchant," Casil was saying. "He trades stuff they bring in from the coast. He has the best collection of knives and swords in Jerusalem! He showed me an Egyptian sword with blue glass swirled into the grip and cross guards carved like snakes with little ruby eyes. It was a beauty!"

"Bronze or iron?" asked Jedan.

"Bronze, but he has iron ones, too. And I saw a big battle-bow that must be from Greece. It came up to here on me!" He held a hand to his chest, winning impressed "Hahs" from his friends.

"What's the guy's name?" asked Josiah.

"Kochesh. He's part Philistine."

"So when can we go?" asked Beriah.

"Tomorrow, after class. We'll get something to eat in the market."

After eating, the boys walked along the path between one end of their building and the garden wall of the girls' building. They heard several girls' choirs practicing together. Each choir was taking a different part in a polyphonic medley. Together they sounded like a thousand harps, lyres, and pipes, weaving a beautiful melody that rolled and bounced along endlessly. Josiah thought of the Kidron brook down the eastern hill. It sang like that, always changing but never saying anything, never repeating itself but never ending.

All four boys turned wordlessly toward an open gate in the wall. They looked in at the courtyard full of girls. Josiah scanned until he located a certain group, then searched each face in turn until he spotted Hannah.

He felt Casil's hand on his shoulder. "I'll get Jarra to come with me to the market tomorrow. You see if Hannah will come with you. Or whoever it is you're hawking at." He grinned slyly at Josiah but was being ignored. Josiah felt his heart race a little as the chorus of choirs fell silent and the leader of Hannah's group gestured to Hannah. It meant she was about to sing a solo!

Some of the choirleaders began talking to their choirs about certain problems. Other choirs started singing a different warm-up song. Hannah's choir leader had her group start a psalm that Josiah recognized as one of Asaph's. The whole choir sang out the first verse. Hannah sang the second.

Out of Zion, the perfection of beauty,
God has shone forth!

Josiah imagined he felt the sun breaking over the horizon by the Mount of Olives at dawn. Something warmed his face, too, just like at dawn. The choir quickly sang the third verse, calling God to come in fire and tempest and judgment and so forth, the kind of things Josiah felt were dwelt on far too much given the kingdom's present state of safety and prosperity.

The choir came to a pause. Other choirs were singing now, making it hard to hear only one. He heard Casil's "Hey, you want to be late?" but ignored him again. He leaned out of the gateway and kept listening to Hannah's choir, hoping to hear her voice again.

I am God, your God.
I do not reprove you for your sacrifices.

Fantastic, thought Josiah sarcastically. *God has no objection to killing lambs and bulls.*

I shall take no young bull from your house,
Nor he-goats from your folds.

An odd thing to say, since He does take our goats and bulls all the time. Dad spends his life taking care of all that goes on for those sacrifices, and he's in the service of God.

For every beast of the forest is mine,
The cattle on a thousand hills.

Even though Hannah had sung this last line as a solo, Josiah was actually thinking about the psalm more than about the singer.

If I hungered, I would not tell you,
For the world is mine, and its fullness.

So why all the blood and burning? Josiah wanted to know. *The Levites probably made it up to keep themselves important.*

"Hey, Josiah, will you quit gaping and come on? She won't leave any time soon." Josiah waved dismissively at Casil and gave him a nasty look. He and the other boys left Josiah at the gateway and walked toward their school building.

> Sacrifice thanksgiving to God,
> Fulfill your vows to the Most High.
> Call on me in the day of trouble,
> I will rescue you, and you will honor me.

Josiah thought about the line "Sacrifice *thanksgiving* to God." Offer thanksgiving as a sacrifice to God. We offer lambs as a sacrifice just like God said to. But why does Asaph's psalm say thanks is a sacrifice?

Johanon had already started the afternoon's music lesson when Josiah, late for the second time that day, slipped into the room and sat down in the back. His thoughts were still over in the girls' courtyard as the lesson began.

"Music is more than just a skill," Johanon was saying. "We never do our best until we project our own feelings through sound. Your soul must give itself entirely to the expression. Music is the issue of the heart as surely as the words you speak. It reveals what is really in you. You may try to lie, but in time it becomes apparent whether your speech is in your heart."

Hardly, thought Josiah. Johanon had always been good to him but the old man didn't quite see life clearly, in Josiah's opinion. *I know I could convince you I was sincere about anything I sang. Even a funeral lament.* He grinned to himself. *Even a love song.* Josiah began singing in his mind a popular song about Jacob working years in order to marry Rachel, the woman he loved. He works against treachery, frustration, and—Josiah caught the teacher's eye and remembered his embarrassment from the morning. He caught up with what Johanon was teaching just in time.

"Josiah, sing the first verse of 'The earth is Jehovah's' to the tune 'Sunrise.'" That was the usual tune. Josiah had been worried his teacher would ask for something strange considering what he had just been saying. Josiah took a breath and relaxed his throat, then sang the verse with its sprightly tune as instructed.

The earth is Jehovah's, and its fullness;
The world, and its inhabitants.

"Good. Now let's hear that same verse to the tune 'Aiyeleth.'"

Oh, here's the trick, moaned Josiah, though he already wanted to laugh. He sang the same triumphant words to the sorrowful, poignant tune of Aiyeleth. The contrast was so sharp the whole class laughed out loud.

"Are you so sorry the earth belongs to Jehovah? Is it such a painful fact to a son of Levi that God rules this world?" Johanon was visibly amused, and everyone, including Josiah, laughed again. "Perhaps you would sing for us the familiar words to that tune, from 'My God, my God'?"

My God, my God, why have you abandoned me?
So far from helping me—the words of my groaning!

Josiah sang the lines well, pouring the feeling of Aiyeleth into the more fitting words. The class was silent this time, though several couldn't help imagining the music of the first psalm matched to the words of the second, an equal incongruity.

"Which words were the right words, and which were the wrong words?" asked Johanon. No one responded for a moment.

"Master Johanon," said one of the better students in the class, beginning as he was supposed to begin everything a student said to his teacher, "the right words went to the right music. The words weren't wrong."

"Even when set to the wrong music?" asked the master.

"Both were from the sacred psalms," offered another student.

"Did the great king David intend for us to sing his psalms to music? Did Jehovah give them to be set to our music?"

The answer to that question was so obviously *Yes,* no one responded. Josiah remembered all the times his teachers asked questions with obvious answers. He wondered why they did that, and what point this teacher was trying to make. After all, they sang all the psalms and other Scriptures besides. Johanon had sung in his own choir in the palace of Jehovah just three weeks ago.

"Do you need our music to understand those words?" Johanon continued. He recited each of the two verses unmusically. "Are you not still happy with 'The earth is,' and sad when you hear the first verse of 'My God, my God'?"

Josiah thought that was just as obvious, but Casil had to interject, "That depends on whether or not I know the ending. David was all happy by the end of the psalm, so maybe I would think of the joyful conclusion when I heard the psalm's first verse and be happy." He looked sincere, but Josiah expected he was just causing trouble. Casil was rarely sincere.

"It is certainly good to know your psalms that well. But I don't believe anyone could read the first twenty-one verses feeling joy. The speaker is clearly one who trusted God but found himself in a horrible strait. Any soul who knows and loves Jehovah finds such a situation painful and torturous." Johanon looked steadily at Casil for a moment before continuing. "If we understand the words without the music, and we have a certain feeling from the words alone, then what happens when we wrap music around the words? Do we still understand them as the great king David intended?"

Josiah finally gave the answer he supposed his teacher wanted. "When the music says the same thing as the words, you understand what David meant." Josiah hoped his answer would get them to practice sooner, for he was tired of instruction for today.

"And what if you match the wrong music to the words?"

"Everyone laughs at you."

"And you don't understand what Jehovah wanted you to understand. You think about how funny it is. Or you miss the meaning entirely." Johanon looked at Casil, but Casil was looking at the ceiling.

Practice went well enough that afternoon. They learned a new arrangement of "O give thanks" with Josiah singing lead. He also was part of a special trio that was to sing at the Levite festival next month. They finished the day with instrumental practice, making a small orchestra of harps, lyres, flutes, pipes, and drums.

When school was over, Master Johanon asked Josiah to stay for a moment. Though he was eager to go slinging with Casil, Josiah enjoyed attention from his teacher and hoped it was something good. He dreaded that it might be about all the times he had been late. Casil and the guys went on to the slinging match while Josiah followed Johanon out of the classroom building and across the street into the Levite craftsmens' building.

They entered one of the small storerooms before Johanon stopped and turned to his student. "I'm looking forward to your entry in the composition contest. I am pleased with your performance this spring. Jehovah has given you a great gift and you are learning to use it well." Josiah never knew what to say to that sort of thing, but he thought something humble was appropriate. "Our God is generous," was his reply.

Johanon contemplated him silently, smiling. "I have another gift for you." He stepped to the side of the room and lifted an object off the floor. When he turned, Josiah saw that it was a harp. "King Solomon's generosity to the musicians allows us to award our more promising students. I hope it meets your approval." He handed the harp to Josiah. Josiah only stared at it, feeling its weight in his hands, not knowing what to say. An instrument of its kind was worth a thousand gold shekels. Only full palace musicians had instruments of that quality. Josiah hadn't expected to own one of his own for ten or fifteen years.

"Thank you," he said quietly. He held up the harp to the sunlight and turned it around admiringly. It was a graceful curve of rich, dark wood with one side enlarged as a sound box. Josiah cradled it in his left arm and braced it against his neck and chest. He drew his right hand across the strings, evoking a sweet, perfectly tuned chord.

"Why?" he asked Johanon.

"Why you? I told you. The king's generosity and your own merit. You can show your appreciation by mastering its use and ministering music in the palace of Jehovah." He stepped closer and gripped Josiah's arm. "Jehovah has put a great gift in you. This device is a tool to bring out that gift. Use it wisely."

Josiah jogged downhill from the western gate of Jerusalem into the valley. He was going to be the last one at the slinging match. After leaving Johanon, he had rushed home to show his parents the harp but they hadn't been there. He had left the harp in the front room and reluctantly went to join his friends. Josiah loved slinging, but he would have stayed and played every song he knew had he not told Casil, Jedan, and Beriah he would meet them.

"This is not your day to be on time, is it?" asked Casil when he saw Josiah trot up. Holding their slings and waiting for Josiah, his friends stood at the base of the ridge that rose across the valley from the western wall of Jerusalem.

"Beriah feels ready," said Jedan. "He told me he was going to beat us all."

"What? I did not," Beriah said, bewildered.

"I think we need to cut his big head down a cubit," Jedan continued.

"Cut me? What did I do?"

"I hear you got a shiny new harp," Casil said to Josiah as the others bantered on.

"Yeah, who told you?" Josiah replied.

"Well, I know lots of things." Casil smiled and looked out at the field of targets they had set up. Different-sized blocks and logs at different distances were worth different values, measured in "shekels."

"Let's get started," Casil announced. He loaded his sling and whirled it over his head, staring out into the field. He suddenly released one end of the strap and snapped his wrist down, sending the palm-sized stone shooting forward. With a loud crack it struck a wooden block. The other three boys cheered and hooted, Beriah calling the slinger talented and the other two calling him lucky.

A shooter could aim at any target he wanted, but a miss wasted his turn. The sloping, stony field in front of them had ten targets of different sizes at varying distances. The boys took turns slinging for a set number of turns. Whoever had the most shekels at the end was the winner.

"Let's see if you can do anything today besides sing a pretty song," Casil taunted Josiah.

Josiah lifted his sling and weighed a smooth round rock in his hand. He held one hand underneath the wide patch sewn into the middle of the sling and placed the rock in the middle of the patch. He then closed his hand on the rock, wrapping the leather patch around it. He turned it over to let the two halves of the strap fall together. Then he slid his other hand along the doubled strap to their ends. One end he wound around his right hand, and the other he gripped tightly in the same hand. He swung the sling backwards and then whirled it over his head once, twice, three times—faster each time. Fixing his eye on a fairly close target, he waited until the stone was pulling away as hard as he wanted, then released the loose end of the strap and snapped his wrist toward the target. His stone shot across the field and glanced off the top of the target with a whap! Casil and the others cheered. "Five shekels!" shouted Casil. "And on his first shot!"

Jedan and Beriah took their shots, and then the second round began. The contest sailed through the second and third rounds. By the time Casil's turn came on the fourth round, he was behind Josiah fifteen shekels. He loaded the sling, whirled it once over his head, then lowered it halfway, spinning it at an angle to his side. He then stepped back with his left foot and waved his arm back and forth in front of him causing the sling to spin in a figure eight. Suddenly he snapped his wrist and shot the stone sidearm, letting the long strap wrap around his body. His stone flashed toward a distant target—and missed by a hand's breadth.

"Good shot, showoff!" yelled Jedan as a chorus of laughs and jeers assaulted Casil, who stalked sullenly backward and sat down. Josiah was laughing at him, too. "That was very impressive," he said. "You should join the army. You could distract the enemy by entertaining them while our men sneak around behind."

A great shot by Jedan left him tied for first at the end of the fourth round. They had just started the last round when a voice behind them called, "You troops need to win this war soon. The sun is almost in." They turned to see a burly soldier walking toward them in full rig with helmet, armor, and sword. "I don't want you terrorizing the countryside after the city gates close." The boys all knew Shammoth, chief guard of the western gate. He got a warm greeting of mild insults and mock salutes.

Shammoth watched round five. Casil, leaving out the antics, redeemed himself with a successful shot at the twenty-five-shekel target he had missed. Josiah was only ten shekels behind, but decided a tie was not good enough. He aimed for a target worth twenty shekels, but he missed. Casil absolutely hooted. "Ha! Stay in school with a harp in your hand! Maybe you can hit something there." Josiah didn't voice his thoughts, not wanting his father to hear from Shammoth what he wanted to say.

They started to head home when Casil challenged Shammoth to take a sling. "I bet you've been sitting in your tower too long to remember what to do with a sling!" the boy taunted, grinning.

"Probably, probably so," sighed Shammoth. "But for the sake of honor, I'll try." The soldier drew his own sling from his belt and picked up a stone much larger than those the Levites had used. "My eyes are weak. Is that a target way out there?" He pointed to their most distant target, a forty-shekel prize no one had hit that evening. It was a cubit-long log, two hand breadths thick, lying horizontally on top of a rock over half a bow-shot away.

Everyone held his breath as Shammoth loaded his sling, braced his legs in an open stance, and whirled the sling levelly over his head. The sunlight was reddish and the air still. Shammoth snapped his wrist. No one saw the stone fly, but there was instantly a sharp crack and burst of white splinters as the little log shattered. The boys erupted in "oohs" and "ohs" at the display. Shammoth looked at them in satisfaction. "Maybe my old bones have a little iron left in them," he said.

Notes to the Reader

Levites and "school" in the tenth century BC

Levi was one of the twelve sons of Israel (Jacob), each of whom fathered one of the twelve tribes of Israel. The descendants of each son were named after their forefather, so the Levites were the descendants of Levi. God distinguished the Levites as the tribe that would take care of the work in the tabernacle and later in the temple, or palace, of Jehovah (Num. 3). They also had a special responsibility to teach God's Word to the rest of the Israelites.

The Levites did not do anything to earn the honor God gave them. In fact, nothing especially good is recorded about Levi himself. On the contrary, he consented with the other brothers to selling Joseph into slavery. Even worse, he and his brother Simeon tricked and slaughtered all the men in an entire city (Gen. 34). Though ostensibly to avenge a crime committed against their sister Dinah, their attack was excessively bloody and may have been motivated as much by greed as a desire for revenge (Gen. 49:5-7).

Furthermore, one of his descendants, Korah, became one of the Bible's most notorious rebels against God (Num. 16). Korah helped lead an attempt to overthrow Moses and Aaron, whom God had made the leaders of Israel. God miraculously demonstrated Korah's error and sent a horrible punishment on all the men who had followed Korah in the uprising. Centuries later the New Testament writer Jude used Korah as an example of what happens to those who falsely claim to speak for God (v. 11).

God elevated the Levites to a position of honor only because He is gracious. He did not give them an allotment in the Promised Land like He did every other tribe. This restriction was in part a punishment, but God actually turned the punishment into a blessing. He scattered them in various cities around Israel and made them teachers of His Word. Though they did not have their own land, they gained the privilege of teaching about God in the lands of every other tribe.

By the time God had King Solomon build the temple, the Levites were numerous. King David organized them into divisions. Many specialized as treasurers, musicians, or gatekeepers (I Chron. 24-26). The prosperity of the kingdom, as well as the Levites' responsibility to keep and teach the Word of God and continue the temple service, makes it very likely they would have developed systematic ways of teaching their young people. Archaeology has provided some evidence of formal education at this time. The "Gezer Calendar" is a small limestone tablet with what appears to be a student's exercise to remember the significance of the months of the year written on it. The tablet had been repeatedly erased and reused repeatedly.

The name *Jehovah*

Most English versions of the Bible represent God's name by writing "lord" in all capital letters. You can see the difference between "Lord" and "LORD." The first word translates a Hebrew word that means *master* or *boss*, the same way "lord" is used in English. It is capitalized when it refers to God. The second word, the one with all caps, translates a Hebrew name for God that is commonly written "Jehovah." Wherever you see "LORD" in an English Bible, the name Jehovah is written in the Hebrew Bible.

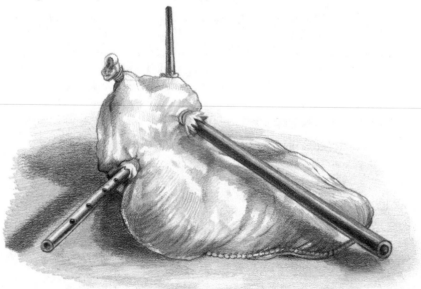

Review and Discussion

1. Describe the setting of Chapter One.

2. Look at the map at the beginning of Chapter One. Describe the significance of Canaan based on its location.

3. How does Josiah feel about the sacrifices? Why does he feel this way?

4. What kind of relationship does Josiah have with his teacher, Johanon?

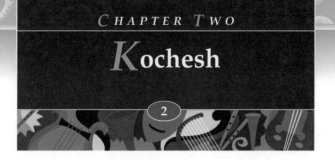

CHAPTER TWO

Kochesh

2

The next day, Josiah awoke to the lightening sky and sleepily looked out over the city. From his rooftop vantage he could see a few people already going about their morning chores. Birds chirped and chattered around him.

To his left and above him the palace of Jehovah loomed in shadow on the top of Mt. Moriah. Farther away down the slope of Moriah stood the great palace of Solomon and the house of the Forest of Lebanon. The Mount of Olives rose behind them, silhouetted by the pre-dawn sky. The sky was clear, so when the sun came out it would surely be—the sun! Josiah pulled himself up, determined to get to school on time for once.

He saw that his younger brother was still asleep and decided that wasn't fair. He grabbed the handle of the ceiling door, yanked it open, and slammed it down. Izhar woke with a start. Josiah, pleased with himself for encouraging his brother to be at school on time, walked down into the house. His room was on the upper floor. After washing up from a bowl of water left last night for that purpose, he dressed, gathered his things, and walked downstairs.

The harp sat on display in one corner of the big room. His parents had come home to find it in the middle of the floor just inside the front door, obviously intended to draw their attention. Josiah's father, Adaiah, had known his son was to receive the award from the chief musicians but had not told anyone else in the family. Josiah had come home from the slinging match to a shower of gushing pride and congratulations from Mom and Dad. Even his brother and sister appeared happy for him.

Josiah walked over to his harp and picked it up carefully. He cradled it in his left arm and ran his right hand over the smooth curve of dark wood. Last night he had played song after song for his family, keeping everyone up past bedtime. His dad had played a little, too, even though the harp was not his strength. Dad's hands weren't made for harping, Josiah thought, smiling to himself.

He drew his own dexterous hand across the strings and played a few measures of "Lion's Voice," a tune with a surprisingly gentle beginning.

"Is music even better than food?" asked a sweet voice. Josiah looked around at his mother and actually felt like giving her a hug. "Hasn't that harp put you in a good spirit!" she teased. "Come eat and get to school on time. Being the best in your class is no excuse to be late every morning."

"They'll take that fancy harp away and give it to someone who's on time and nice to his brother," called Izhar, walking sleepily into the kitchen in search of nourishment.

As the boys ate bread, honey, and cream, their mother asked what plans they had for the day. "After school I'm going down to the river for a while; it's finally hot enough," reported Izhar, speaking around a mouthful of food.

"Try not to drown," said Josiah. The river was the Kidron, to the east of Jerusalem, and hardly waist-deep on Izhar at its deepest.

"What about your day? Any special diversions?" Mom asked Josiah.

"Right after lunch we—" Josiah hesitated because he wasn't sure how detailed he wanted to be about something Casil planned. "We are going down to the market for a while."

"Who is 'we'?"

"Casil and me and maybe some other guys."

"Well, whatever Casil suggests, don't do it." Josiah glanced at his mom, who grinned back at him. "You need to wipe your chin," she said. "And keep your cousin from hurting himself or disgracing all Levites. And be home early enough to let your sister play that new harp before her bedtime. She nearly went wild last night."

She'll probably break a string, Josiah groaned silently as he finished eating and got up to leave. Noemi, too young to go to school yet, was still fast asleep upstairs.

"Here, take this. Your father and I think a small celebration is in order." She dropped into Josiah's hand five gold coins. "Since you're going to market anyway, you can buy yourself something. Or something for somebody else." She grinned again and Josiah reddened. Izhar's eyes widened, but his mouth was too full to speak clearly.

Josiah strapped on his shoes, gathered his satchel and harp, and headed out the door. Izhar came rushing out behind him, still chewing. Their mother stood in the door watching them go, praying to Jehovah to bring them back safely from another day.

The morning passed slowly. Josiah spent more thought time envisioning the swords, helmets, and armor he would see at the Philistine's shop than concentrating on his lessons. By lunchtime he was ready for a break and an adventure.

"Come on, can't we eat in the market?" Casil called to his friends. Josiah didn't like eating while he walked, but he'd gotten good at it of necessity. He, Jedan, Beriah, Hannah, and Rachel, a friend of Hannah's, followed Casil out of the Levite area down the west slope of Mt. Moriah past the royal residences to Ophel. The marvelous government buildings and residences of the wealthy towered over the narrow street. Hundreds of brightly dressed people bustled everywhere.

A peal of trumpets ahead announced an important person's approach. The crowd parted from the main street to let a mounted processional pass. Five Israelite honor guards rode before a litter carried by twelve burly slaves. A retinue of servants and subordinates followed. On the litter was a man robed in bright white and red with a golden crown on his turban. "The king of Dedan! Make way for the king of Dedan!" shouted the lead guard. They watched as the procession passed them, heading uphill.

"Hey, they're turning short of the palace. I wonder if they are going to one of the queens' houses?" said Casil. After passing the six friends, the short parade had turned right, leaving the main road for a side street that led to a block of private houses overlooking the eastern wall.

"Isn't King Solomon married to a daughter of Dedan?" asked Rachel.

"Probably," answered Jedan. "It seems like they announce a new queen every other month."

"Being a queen must be great!" Rachel sighed. "You get all these beautiful robes, jewels, servants to do everything for you, delicious food . . . "

"You don't look like you're suffering from a famine," broke in Casil. Rachel swiped at his hair, causing him to jump out of the way and laugh. She chased him for two laps around Beriah before deciding to spare the antagonist's life again. Casil teased her regularly, but he tried to stay out of reach when he made her angry. Rachel wasn't fat, but she wasn't small, either.

"You're just hurt that Jarra wouldn't come with you," Jedan taunted Casil. "Women's feelings are a lot more important whenever she's around."

"She went home for lunch," Casil replied shortly.

They continued down the hill from Ophel, passing through the gate in the old city wall into Jerusalem's old quarter. King David had captured the Canaanite fortress of Jebus more than fifty years earlier. Located on a rocky ridge bounded by the Kidron Valley to the east and the western valley Israelites simply called The Valley, it was a highly secure location inhabited since ancient times. The only easy approach was across the Ophel, from the north. This route allowed enough traffic to flow that the city could function as capital of the kingdom without compromising its security. David had renamed it the City of David, strengthened its fortifications, rebuilt its buildings, and kept his throne there some thirty years.

King Solomon had extended the city wall around an area twice the size of David's city. He had made Ophel and Mt. Moriah, where the great palace of Jehovah now stood, part of the city. The wealth of Solomon's flourishing kingdom was reflected in the opulent palaces and government buildings covering the new city. Jerusalem, the city's traditional name, had become its common designation since the death of David.

The main road curved gently right as they walked into the heart of the old city. The old city had undergone some renovation in the last ten years. Key buildings now rose three and four stories high. As the city became more and more of an international crossroads, even the older sections became vital centers of business and commerce. The main marketplace had not only remained in the old city but had grown into the richest trade center west of the Euphrates.

The large building that formed the corner of the market rose beside them. Four spacious stories high, it housed three well-known families of money-lenders along with dozens of servants. It was so wide, it must have surrounded an interior courtyard. The bottom level on two sides presented various-sized offices where people might buy gold and silver, borrow money, or enlist wealthy support for a commercial or political venture.

Walking with his friends down the lane between the corner building, called the Block, and its neighbor, Josiah looked over the men sitting and talking in successive shops. They were richly dressed, confident, at ease with the world. Josiah was awed to think that many of these men could have simply bought a harp like the one of which he was so proud.

Jerusalem's marketplace opened before them at the end of the alley. As the six friends entered, sounds and smells dramatically different than their peaceful Levite school assaulted them. Brilliant colors sang across banners, canopies, and clothing of people from all parts of Israel and neighboring lands. The distinctive blue-trimmed white robes all Levites wore looked bland in the midst of such varied hues. Fortunately, there were enough Levites scattered around the market to keep them from looking conspicuous.

Canopies shielded the bustling crowd of people from the midday sun. Casil was already working through the crowd, heading toward the far side of the market where their destination lay, but Beriah interrupted with a booming, "Can we eat first, please?"

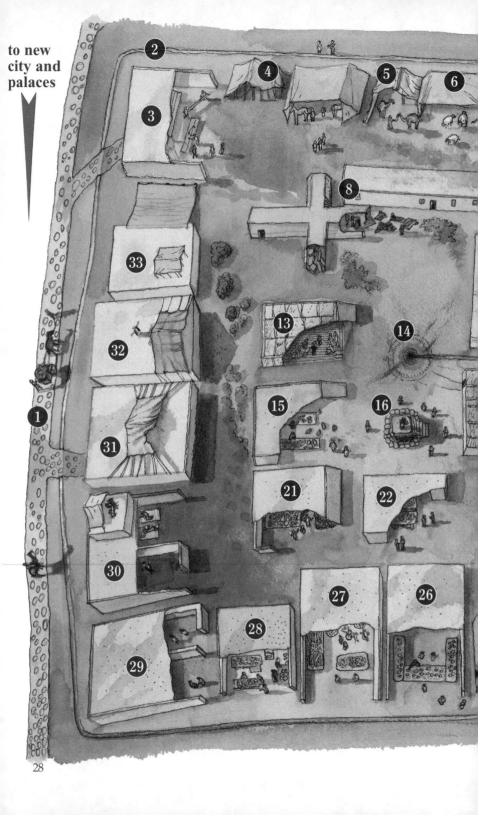

to new
city and
palaces

28

Jerusalem Marketplace

1. Main Road
2. Drainage Ditch
3. Carpenter Shop
4. Horses and Exotic Animals
5. Camel Dealer
6. Sheep & Cattle
7. Tanner's Bazaar
8. Clothier
9. Iron & Metal Works
10-12. Potters
13. Rug/Carpet Dealer Housing
14. Water Drain
15. Baker
16. Public Forum (Court of Address)
17. Gold Dealer
18-20. Foreign Imports
21-28. Fresh Produce & Other Farm Products
29-33. Merchant Housing

29

Though Casil looked annoyed, food sounded good to everyone else, too. Besides, the eating bazaar was just to their left. Down the row of shops was a place offering cooked meats for hungry marketers. Jedan gave one of his eight coins in exchange for ten roasted quails, treating his friends. The girls ate one each and the boys took two each. Beriah gathered every scrap they left and then bought himself a honeyed wheat loaf. Josiah, who had hardly eaten half his second quail, remembered seeing Beriah once eat eleven barley loaves and an entire cake of figs at one meal.

Finishing their lunch, they followed the impatient Casil out of the court of the eating bazaar and turned left. The fresh produce bazaar was on one side and the halls of the food merchants on the other. Though vast quantities of grain, oil, and wine passed through the latter every day, Josiah was much more interested in the fresh produce stalls. He looked over at the rows of neatly arranged fruits and vegetables, wishing they could wander up and down them. Past the stalls, a flash of metal and a flurry of fighting men caught his attention. The second building of produce vendors blocked his sight. He hurried past it and looked down the next alley. The crowd kept him from seeing clearly, but he saw two men on a raised platform and a flash of red and white.

Josiah rushed ahead and called for Casil's attention. "Let's go see what's happening in there," he yelled over the noise.

"Where? Why?" Casil demanded. He followed Josiah's pointing finger down the third alley, but kept walking.

"What are they doing?" asked Josiah.

"How would I know?" returned Casil.

"Let's go find out!" He gripped Casil's arm and pulled him down the last alley on the block. They walked between the last row of fresh produce and the back of the huge exporters' display house into the Court of Address, the northern half of the innermost court of the marketplace.

"That's Kochesh!" exclaimed Casil. The boys had joined a ring of spectators around a most unusual scene. Up on the platform from which messengers gave public announcements three men engaged in what looked like a battle. Two, armed with sword and shield, fenced with one another. The third, armed only with a tambourine, danced around them playing a martial tune. Two drummers and a flutist played along from the side. Josiah almost laughed at the absurdity, but the combatants were too obviously in earnest for it to be a big joke.

"Who's Kochesh?" he finally asked Casil. "The daysman?"

"Yeah, the daysman. Or whatever he is." The dancing tambourinist did not appear to be refereeing the fight as a daysman would. He darted around and even between the fighters. But suddenly one swordsman scored a ringing hit on his opponent's breastplate. Kochesh raised his arms and gave a victory cry, stepping between the opponents. The crowd cheered and the drummers broke into a victory beat.

Kochesh slapped the winner on the back and held up a sheathed sword someone handed him. Making a quick motion with his free hand, he started into a song.

Who is the man with a strong hand,
The man who can swing an iron sword?

The crowd responded in chorus,

With speed like an eagle
And strength like an ox,
A mighty man swings an iron sword!

Another round of cheering turned into a hum of conversation as Kochesh presented the sheathed sword to the victor. He and an assistant collected the blunt swords and practice armor into a heap beside the platform.

"Come on," ordered Casil and pushed his way forward. He and Josiah made their way to where Kochesh stood talking. "Kochesh! This is Josiah, the son of Adaiah, whom I told you about."

Josiah looked into the bright eyes of a tall and handsome man about thirty years old. As he bowed, Josiah took in the colorful red and white robes that marked Kochesh as a man of some means. "So this is the great musician? I'll have to hear your song sometime." Kochesh followed his words with such a warm smile Josiah couldn't help smiling back.

"What is the sword-fighting for?" asked Casil.

"Are these more of your friends?" Kochesh nodded to Jedan, Beriah, Hannah, and Rachel, who had walked up behind them. Casil made some quick introductions and repeated his question, but Kochesh first had to find out all about the others. He seemed pleased that they were training to be musicians. Finally, he explained the reason for the mock combat and his peculiar role.

"People enjoy it. Everyone likes watching, and some enjoy participating. I make fine new friends. They will know who I am when we meet again. And by acting the mad daysman I make the match more exciting to the crowd."

"What kind of sword did you give the winner?" Casil wanted to know.

"A good iron sword, of course. The prize for a winner is an iron sword."

"Whom do I have to beat?"

"Oh, you want to get on the platform? Do they teach you more than music in that priests' school?"

"I'm a pretty good swordsman," asserted Casil. Kochesh laughed and asked whom Casil would like to fight.

"What are my choices? Who was the man who just lost?"

"A friend of the winner. I welcome any participant. Only, no one who loses can compete again. You find your own opponent. I ask only that any match provide a good show for the watchers."

"And the prize is another sword? Like the one you just gave away?"

"Yes. An iron sword for the hand of a mighty man." Kochesh's eyes danced playfully, daringly. Casil looked at the platform and then back to Kochesh. Josiah saw it coming.

"I'll fight Josiah here. I know he'd like a chance at winning a free sword."

"No thank you," Josiah was already saying. "Find someone else to bruise." He laughed a little. "Jedan will fight you, or maybe Beriah will wrestle you for—"

"Nonsense!" interrupted Casil. "This is your chance to pay me back for outshooting you yesterday. And one of us gets it, whatever happens," he said, meaning the prize sword. "We'll be your next match, Kochesh!"

"We'll have at it, then!" shouted Kochesh as he leaped up on the platform and struck his tambourine. The other minstrels joined in and summoned the crowd's attention. Casil was already putting on the leather armor. Josiah felt his stomach tighten as he looked at all the people watching. He felt like there were thousands of them. Jedan was beside him, grinning. Josiah glanced at Hannah, who appeared confused. *Oh well,* he thought. *It's just a game.*

He joined Casil at the pile of armor and began strapping on the heavy tunic. "This is great!" Casil remarked. "One of us gets a sword from his merchandise, free. You feel like being beaten?"

Josiah flushed as he buckled on the tough leather skirt. "I just ate," he complained.

"Two stout young men want to test their valor," announced Kochesh. He held another sheathed sword over his head and sang,

> Who is the man with a strong hand,
> The man who can swing an iron sword?

The audience sang out their reply. Casil had his armor on and stepped up onto the platform. The drummers immediately let out a loud roll and someone blew a trumpet sharply. The audience roused and started stamping and calling. Had he been at a distance, Josiah would have thought them merely excited, but at the center of attention he felt like a rabbit in a ring of wild dogs.

Stepping up on the platform in full view of all, Josiah felt his heart pounding. A young man helped him grip his shield and sword, then stepped aside. Kochesh stood between him and Casil, his arms up, singing a taunt song to his crowd.

> Hear, ye people, do you seek a man?

A champion to guide you, O Jerusalem?

About twenty people joined in the response:

> Give us a leader to bind and plant,
> Of iron, a breaker; of song, a dove.

> Hear the song, O people,
> And see the iron in the hand of a man.

With that, Kochesh dropped his arms and stepped aside. The drums started a pulsating beat. Josiah looked at the figure before him advance with a raised sword. Startled into action, he quickly brought up his shield and squared his stance.

Casil led with his sword, flicking and jabbing at Josiah's face. Josiah shoved his shield forward and then slashed at Casil with an uppercut. They traded rapid blows to each other's shield. Josiah missed and threw himself off balance, narrowly dodging a thrust at his head. Before he could recover, Casil rammed his shield into Josiah's chest, knocking him backwards and nearly off the edge of the platform. Josiah looked up at his cousin, who had jumped back to gather himself for another charge. Suddenly a flurry of red and white swept between them. Kochesh struck his tambourine. "We must have a clean hit. No shoving men over the side," he said. Josiah got to his feet and walked sideways to the middle of their makeshift arena. He was surprised to notice how loud the crowd was above the ruckus of Kochesh's music group. Another rattle of the tambourine and Kochesh resumed the fight. Casil led with his shield this time, his sword ready. Josiah stepped forward and raised his shield, then spun around on his left foot and swung his sword backhanded at Casil. His slash was blocked with a clang of metal and a jar to his shoulder. Josiah stopped a quick thrust with his shield, then struck again.

The two circled twice, stabbing and slashing, each trying to catch an opening. Josiah thought of a good move, and tried it. He swung his sword in a sweeping overhand. Casil raised his shield to block and readied a counter thrust. But Josiah brought his sword down halfway through its arc and tried to slip it under Casil's upheld shield. He just missed Casil's side, but Casil brought the edge of his own shield down hard on Josiah's arm and hacked Josiah's left thigh with his edgeless sword. Josiah hit him hard with his shield, knocking them apart.

Josiah was furious. Pain knifed through his arm and leg while spots danced in his vision. The crowd's shouting filled his ears. For once, he rushed at Casil, leading with the sword. Casil poised his shield, then quickly shifted his body sideways and aimed his sword. He parried Josiah's thrust and struck him smartly in the center of the chest. Josiah staggered backwards. He caught his breath and wanted to shove his blade right through Casil, but Kochesh was between them again. Josiah realized he had lost, and the crowd was cheering for the winner, Casil. As Kochesh congratulated the victor and awarded him a sword, the same man who had helped Josiah into his armor helped him remove it.

It was the time of day after lunch when most everyone had eaten and wanted to go indoors away from the heat, and probably catch a nap. Consequently no one else had felt like sword-fighting, and the crowd dissolved. Kochesh gladly invited them all to visit his shop.

The northwest strip of the outer ring of the market was made up mostly of foreign importers. Kochesh led them to a three-story building decorated with Tyrian symbols. After entering a narrow doorway, they walked up a staircase of acacia wood into a spacious chamber on the second story.

The shiny wooden floor was partly covered in colorful rugs. The room was decorated in shades of blue and green with white trim. Everywhere metal gleamed from spears, swords, and armor. Beside the military hardware were expensive brass and silver mirrors and, to Josiah's surprise, a collection of musical instruments.

The group wandered around the room gazing at the wares. Casil walked to a display of armor. There were polished bronze breastplates, iron helmets painted or covered in silver, bronze guards for the shins and forearms, and wide leather girdles. All were finely carved and decorated. A few had gemstones inlaid. They appeared to all be imported from other lands, including Egypt, Anatolia, Aram, and Greece. Casil stared in awe at the beautiful collection.

Beriah handled a spear with a long, thick shaft and a large bronze head. It was ornately carved and banded with bronze. Jedan was trying out a short Hittite iron sword. Rachel admired some of the jewelry, fingering blue and yellow stones set in a gold bracelet. Hannah went to the musical instruments and looked over them for a moment, then selected a light wooden pipe. Josiah watched from behind as she examined it carefully and then raised it to her lips. Blowing gently above the aperture, she generated a high, sweet tone without any waver.

"Do you know its origin?" Josiah asked her.

"No," Hannah replied. "I haven't seen anything quite like it. All of these instruments look foreign. They must be worth a lot."

"They are indeed worth much in the hands of one whose skill is equal to their craftsmanship." The two Levites turned to see Kochesh smiling at them. "I suspect the lady is such a one. Would she honor us with a short melody?" Hannah flushed and looked down, but after some encouragement from Josiah she spread her hands carefully over the few holes on the pipe and played a simple, cheerful tune.

"It's beautiful," Hannah said as she lowered the pipe. "Where are these flutes from?"

"Upper Egypt," Kochesh informed her. "I understand they use material from far south, from Ethiopia. The purity of their tone is unsurpassed."

Josiah picked up another instrument, a sort of lyre made of a broad sound box and two parallel arms with strings between them. The front of the sound box was etched and painted with a subtle image Josiah thought was a face, but he couldn't tell whether it portrayed a human or an animal.

"That's a Grecian lover's lyre," Kochesh offered. "Do you know how to play?"

Josiah replied that he was familiar with stringed instruments, but confessed he had never played a lover's lyre, Grecian or otherwise. Kochesh laughed and offered to demonstrate. Taking the elegant instrument from Josiah, he strung the strings and tightened them, then knelt down to play. Resting on one knee, he gripped the far arm at its base and pressed it against his raised knee, holding the lyre close across his body. "You embrace it, then caress it," he said, folding his right arm around the top of the lyre and drawing his hand across and down the strings, his fingers nimbly playing a lively opening tune. He continued into a soft, sweet strain. The music became more dissonant, increasing in tempo and swelling to a climax, then ending in a rich resolution.

The Levites, musicians all, had ears to appreciate the skill that Kochesh had displayed. Josiah had held his breath from the point when the dissonance entered until the resolution; he was completely caught up in the emotions of the music. Even as silence fell in the room, he felt his throat tighten with joy.

"Doesn't she have a beautiful voice?" Kochesh asked as he ran his hands down the arms of the lyre. He rose to his feet and faced his audience. Four other customers had listened to his solo appreciatively. Kochesh engaged them in conversation with all the charm of a gentleman.

Josiah looked them over. There was an older and apparently wealthy couple and a pair of men, one obviously a foreigner. The woman held a fine piece of jewelry studded with rubies. As Josiah watched them talk, he wondered what sort of clientele frequented an unmarked shop offering weapons, jewelry, and musical instruments. *I suppose he may just bring in whatever he can find of high value,* he thought. Many merchants were still very eclectic in their offerings.

Noticing that he and his friends were now the objects of their conversation, Josiah strained to hear what they were saying but could not. He turned to the nearest wall to avoid looking like he was eavesdropping. Instantly his attention was distracted. In front of him was a display of swords arranged in a symmetric pattern. The display contained a variety of short and long iron swords with polished blades and carved hilts, but right in the center of them was one that called for all of Josiah's attention.

About a cubit and a half long, its blade gleamed like a mirror and its hilt was of a shiny black stone trimmed in gold. Its aesthetic appeal to Josiah lay less in its decoration than in its form;

blade and hilt were blended so perfectly it looked almost like a leaf. The sharp blade had a delicate etching that matched the gold trim on the hilt. No blemish was visible.

Kochesh had released his older customers and noticed the young Levite admiring a sword. "Please take it down and give it a try. I think you will like its feel." Josiah complied. The sword felt just right in his hand, solid but not cumbersome. He held it up to the sunlight. He waved it in slow circles to feel its balance. It was worth more than the prize sword Kochesh had given Casil.

"Does your eye for merchandise extend from musical instruments to armaments?" asked Kochesh.

"Music is more my place, but this sword is great," came the reply.

"Levites still learn war along with worship, as you showed." said Kochesh. "Here, let me show you something."

Kochesh bowed and took the weapon from Josiah, holding it in his left hand. Picking up a date with his right hand, he held his sword arm straight out at the elbow and bent his wrist, dropping the sword behind his left shoulder. He tossed the date straight up. The sword flashed through the air, but the date didn't even twitch. Kochesh caught the fruit intact in his right hand.

Casil chided him, "Oh, try again. Quit fooling us." Kochesh partly opened his hand, allowing exactly one half of the date to fall free onto the table.

Six surprised Levites stared at the halved date and its grinning divider, who offered one half to Josiah and the other to Casil. After wiping the sword on a cloth he returned it to its wall mount. "It's a good blade. Top quality Hittite iron, made by a master armorer of the royal guild. Please, everyone, come and join me for refreshment." He moved toward a corner of his shop with two broad windows and a ring of couches.

Josiah looked around and noticed that the pair of men had gone. The older couple stood at the far end of the room, facing away from him and talking in low tones. No one else was in the shop. He and his friends settled on the couches with Kochesh, accepting some fruit he offered from a clay bowl.

"Tell me about yourselves," Kochesh instructed. "Casil mentioned that he had some friends he wanted to bring, friends who would enjoy a look at my modest wares. You look like an able and educated group. And not entirely unpleasant to the eye." He nodded to the two girls, who both laughed a little.

"Hear that? He thinks you're cute," Jedan said to Beriah, thumping the big boy's arm and getting a round of laughter from them all.

"Are you a musician as well as these other worthies?" Kochesh asked Jedan, who said he was. "What instruments have they taught you?"

"Mostly the harps, but also pipes and the drums and cymbals, of course."

"I know the lady plays beautifully upon the pipe. Perhaps I should have you play as a band for me. Are you all equally trained?"

Rachel spoke up with, "We're not all quite as good as Josiah."

"The swordsman is also the master minstrel? Splendid! Do they teach you to compose music up on that walled hill, or do you just repeat such tunes as your elders pass on to you?"

Josiah answered, "We compose plenty. We have a composition contest every year and the older students compose even more. The palace musicians like to use new music to sing the psalms."

"Ah, the great palace of Jehovah and its famed Levite musicians. What a life of bliss and ease you must have! To pray and offer sacrifices and make music all the time, getting paid handsomely for it out of the king's treasury."

The kids muttered disagreement. "We spend all our time going to school, practicing, going to the services, working around the palace and the Levite buildings," Casil protested. "We hardly have any time to ourselves. And none of the king's money makes it down to us, I tell you!"

Kochesh looked concerned. "Truly? I'm sorry to hear that. But that is the way of the world; the young bear the burdens while their elders reap the rewards. But, Josiah, let me hear one of these tunes you have composed, if it isn't troublesome to you. You don't have to be back in school today, I hope? No? Then take an instrument of your liking and play for me as if I were Jehovah himself!" Josiah was taken aback by Kochesh's irreverence, but he rose and walked to the display of instruments. The lyre Kochesh had played sat there, but Josiah chose a harp more familiar in design.

Raising the harp to his shoulder, he noticed it was almost as high in quality as his gift harp. Josiah concentrated on the flow of chords in the beginning of his version of "I Will Love Thee." He had composed it to feel like a sunrise, giving thanks to Jehovah for rescuing him from darkness and leading him to a beautiful new day. It opened with the declaration of love to Jehovah, then had some discord to represent the floods of darkness. Next it painted a picture of a growing light, as a single high note represented the first ray of hope, and an increasingly complex melody portrayed the Lord coming and saving him from the sorrows. It concluded with the hymn of joy. Finishing, Josiah returned the harp to its place and faced his host.

"Very, very impressive," beamed Kochesh. "You will be a fine palace singer. Would you mind if I played your piece?"

"I don't have a written score with me," apologized Josiah.

"Oh, not necessary," Kochesh answered. He stood and came to Josiah's side, took up the same harp, and to Josiah's surprise played the opening accurately. "Now that works, but you could increase the tension and expectation with just a little modification." Kochesh played it again, but added more dissonance, causing the music to become very disturbing and almost gripping. Josiah was amazed at the merchant's ability to improvise.

Kochesh continued into the section about the dawn but added extra flourishes that changed Josiah's simple, lilting melody, giving it a more dramatic mood. He somehow wove the discord into the rest of the song, creating a marvelous contrast between the two feelings.

"How did you learn to compose and play like that?" Josiah asked as Kochesh finished.

"There are places other than Jerusalem that know the secrets of music," he laughed. "In my home are true masters who can use any kind of music in any way you wish. Your Levite teachers are adept at one kind of music, but there are as many kinds of music as there are clouds in the sky. It is the language of the heavens, pure feeling flowing through the air, and just like any language it can carry a message."

"Where are you from? What masters are you talking about?"

Kochesh smiled and looked away as if treasuring a memory. "Ashkelon will always be my home, however far the service of Jehovah takes me."

"Ashkelon? So you are a Philistine after all. You don't talk like one."

"My father was an honorable man of Ashkelon, my mother a sweet lady from Gezer and daughter of Judah. I therefore learned both manners of speech and both manners of living. It is my privilege to bring understanding to my two peoples, the children of Philistia and the children of Israel."

"You're half Philistine?"

"I prefer to say I am all Philistine and all Israelite. Two peoples in one person!" They rejoined Josiah's friends. No one else was in the shop now. Josiah was curious to learn more about this unusual man, but Kochesh continued talking. "My soul's desire is that young people such as yourself understand other people and overcome the unfortunate divisions that separate us. I believe Jehovah has chosen me to help unify all His people."

"Then why are you a merchant?" asked Jedan.

"Commerce affords me the means and motive to travel among different nations. Likewise, it offers a door to discussing other cultures. Look at yourselves; did you come to hear me talk, or to see exotic imports? So will many people be persuaded to your side sooner when they have an enticement to hear your arguments."

"How did you get so good at music?" asked Josiah.

"The same way you will. Good teachers, practice, hard work."

"I've never heard anyone who can do some of those things. We don't learn to make up music like that. Are there a lot of men in Ashkelon who can play like you can?"

"There are others. Anyone can learn, though, especially men and women who have as much talent and training as you. Even I can teach you." He folded his hands and leaned forward.

"Music is the way we speak directly to another soul. I can speak to you in three different languages, making very different sounds but meaning the same thing. Now, you understand all of my meaning only if you know the language just as I do. For example," and here he spoke a sentence in Aramaic, the common language for trade and diplomacy. Israelite schools taught it and some people in Jerusalem spoke it. Josiah caught a few words and concentrated to make sense of them.

"Wait, what does that mean?" asked a bewildered Beriah.

"Don't you know? Perhaps I could be more emphatic." He raised a fist and shouted the Aramaic words again so angrily and forcefully Hannah caught her breath. "Ah. You obviously are uneducated," Kochesh continued. He said something else in a very different language with more staccato sound. He looked inquisitively, as if waiting for a response.

"Was that Egyptian?" wondered Casil.

Kochesh nodded. He then smiled broadly and repeated the sentence, raising his arms and finishing with a loud laugh.

"What are you saying?" Rachel demanded.

"I first asked in Aramaic if anyone would like a honey cake, but no one responded. I then commented in Egyptian that I hate Levites and threatened to kill all of you if you don't leave at once. Yet here you remain, accepting neither my hospitality nor reacting to my threats."

"Why was threatening to kill us so funny?" asked Beriah.

"Moron, he was showing how you get a feeling from what people say totally apart from what the words mean."

"Exactly, Casil. But Beriah is no moron; he reacted as most people would have. The way I look and sound means something apart from the words. In a similar way, music carries feeling without words. I can show you how to say all kinds of things with your music."

Kochesh looked around at the group. Josiah wondered again at the strange man who could do so much and was obviously wealthy. *Why is this fellow interested in us?* He wondered what Jedan thought.

"Are you all coming to the youth festival?" Kochesh asked them. He was returned blank looks. "The festival on the evening of the fifth day next week? I'm sorry if you didn't know, but it's difficult to get the word around. Every month there is a festival for youth outside of the city. Anyone is welcome, especially those who are musically inclined. It's a good time to relax and get away from school and home for a while and have some fun before the Sabbath and the new week."

"How many people come?" Jedan asked.

"Four or five hundred."

"What all do you do? Why are musicians welcome?"

"Everyone is welcome, but good music makers can play for the rest of us. They would love to have a group like you. If you can't come next week, perhaps next month. Would you like to look at any more of my goods before you have to go?"

After asking a few prices they realized just how exclusive a shop Kochesh ran. For the suit of Greek armor, he asked two hundred gold shekels; for the sword Josiah liked, sixty; for the musical instruments, seven hundred and higher. Kochesh would come down on those prices a little, Josiah knew, but they were still steep. He thought of the fifty shekels in his pouch. He just might be able to talk the merchant down ten.

Picking the sword back up and showing renewed admiration to draw attention, Josiah began the bartering process by which all business was done from the daily to the international level. He told Kochesh how much he liked it and wanted it, but lamented that money was so hard to come by for a student. Kochesh sympathized and asked how much he could produce. Thirty for sure, maybe forty, if I sacrifice, Josiah calculated. The price might be lowered to fifty since Josiah was such an expert musician, Kochesh conceded. Sensing victory, Josiah proposed to buy the sword by going in debt to his parents if the price came down just five more shekels. Kochesh agreed to take a small loss on the sword since Josiah liked it so much and appreciated good value when he saw it. Satisfied, Josiah produced his five gold coins. Grinning, Kochesh took his money, returned him five shekels change, and gave him the sword in its smooth black leather sheath.

"You had fifty gold shekels with you?" exclaimed Casil as he and the other boys admired Josiah's acquisition. "Where did you come by that?"

"It was a gift," Josiah replied.

Notes to the Reader

Semitic Poetry and Music

The poetry of Israel and its neighboring countries did not rhyme the way English poetry normally does. While English poetry rhymes sounds, Semitic poetry rhymes ideas. Ideas may repeat, contrast with each other, or build on one another. The Book of Psalms is a collection of Semitic poetry; Hebrew psalms contain little more rhyme than their English translations, but the connection of ideas is easy to follow in any language.

Musical lyrics are nearly always poetic. Ancient peoples admired song as a way to entertain and educate. Great religious epics were written in poetry and probably sung publicly to teach young people proper religious beliefs.

Though few instruments have survived from the ancient world, there is ample evidence of what they were like in records and drawings. String instruments were the most common. These included harps, lyres, lutes, and zithers. There is no evidence that bowing was invented. Strings were either struck or plucked. Percussion instruments encompassed drums, cymbals, and various noisemakers like rattles. All of these existed in great variety of shapes and sizes. Drums were made of stretched skins, while cymbals were metal. Air instruments existed, notably horns, reed pipes, and flutes.

Ancient Near Eastern Architecture

Climate and technology governed architecture in the ancient world. Relatively warm and dry weather made thick walls comfortable. Roofs did not have to be sloped since snow was extremely rare. Instead, the flat roof became another floor of the house, one on which a family could have a measure of privacy with enough light to enjoy a relaxing atmosphere in the cool of the evening.

Light was a major factor in building design because no widespread source of artificial light was available, other than fire.

Windows in the thick walls let in sunlight. But windows needed to be in at least two walls to give sufficient light all day. The resulting architecture consisted of narrow buildings that housed rooms with at least two exterior walls. To make an extremely long building was impractical (it took too long to walk from one part to another). Therefore, buildings of any size had to be square or rectangular, surrounding an open interior courtyard. The courtyard became commonplace, an ideal setting for finding solitude, holding family gatherings, and raising a garden.

Technology limited the height of buildings. Cobblestone construction, used in Israel up through the time of David, did not allow for buildings more than two stories high. Anything higher would have been unstable and would have collapsed. With the development of cut stones that distributed their weight evenly upon the stones below them, walls could be safely built two and three times as high.

Review and Discussion

1. Describe the economic and political conditions in Israel at the time of the story.

2. Why do you suppose the palace of Jehovah was near the palace of Solomon?

3. Why was Kochesh holding a fencing contest in the middle of the marketplace?

4. For what reason did Casil challenge Josiah to the fencing match?

5. What does Kochesh want the friends to think about their Levite teachers?

6. Of all the things Kochesh says about music, are any of them incorrect? If so, which ones?

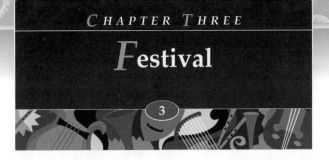

CHAPTER THREE

Festival

3

"Ha!" yelled Adaiah as he struck at his opponent's chest. Josiah barely deflected the sword thrust and twisted out of the way. Another blow fell immediately, throwing him off balance. He swung his round shield at the assailant, clumsily but hard enough to knock him backward. Josiah steadied his feet and raised his sword. Adaiah lunged toward him. Swords and shields clattered together rapidly as each tried to be quick enough to get a stroke through the other's defense. Their swords met with a jarring force. Josiah lost his grip and brought up his shield as he grabbed for the sword, but a stabbing pain under his left armpit told him the fight was over.

"Slain!" cried Adaiah triumphantly. "That's a mortal wound for sure!"

"Don't gloat, Dad," returned Josiah as he bent over, waiting for the pain to lessen. *One fine day,* he thought, *I'm going to beat him in a fair fight.*

"I just wanted you to admit defeat before I lost my wind and died on the spot. You're getting quicker all the time."

Their battleground was a courtyard formed inside a rectangular block of ten square two-story houses, theirs being to one side. Many such blocks made up the short river of brick and stone housing that ran between the outer wall of the palace and the massive western city wall. Hundreds of the poorer Levites lived there. Thousands more lived north of the palace, all dedicated to maintaining its routine ministry.

Father and son laid aside their wooden practice swords and unstrapped the leather armor. They made a sorry sight, sweating and panting, but Josiah's mother could not have been more proud. She watched them talk and laugh and wondered how well they would get along as Josiah got older. Adaiah was a brawny, practical man who loved ordinary people. They had spent the first years of their marriage in the north ministering among the simple farmers of Naphtali near Ramah and Hazor. At that distance from Jerusalem it was easy to lose a sense of the reality of the tabernacle of Jehovah and His presence with Israel. Many people never made the weeklong journey to the capital even for the Day of Atonement. It was a slow labor getting them to understand that being the people of Jehovah was a matter of the heart and not something they were born with.

Moving to Jerusalem to minister in the newly built palace of Jehovah had been a great honor to Adaiah but a melancholy loss of rural work he loved. His wife, knowing him better than anyone else, was sure he would return to the country right away if not for the children. The opportunities they had to learn from the best teachers in Israel were too valuable to lose, especially considering Josiah's exceptional talent. Though Adaiah sometimes had trouble understanding his son, he loved him dearly and wanted the best for him.

"Have you killed our son?"

"No, Laubi, he nearly killed me. Are we ready to eat yet?"

"Yes, of course, but you and Josiah need to wash first. Don't touch me!" She evaded his attempt to throw a sweaty arm around her and ran toward the house with her husband chasing her, demanding affection.

Josiah laughed and, embarrassed, looked around to see if anyone was watching his parents' antics. Someone was; across the small courtyard in the window of a neighbor's house a woman was chuckling merrily. Josiah hastily went inside and found the water basin. He bathed and put on a clean robe.

Josiah sat that evening thinking about the upcoming composition contest. He played through in his mind what he had written, what he had performed for Kochesh. He remembered how Kochesh had changed and added to his composition, hearing and feeling the tension. How could he improve that piece? It was good, but it didn't really surprise a person or bring a tear to one's eye. Josiah hoped it was good enough to win, but he knew it was nothing that would ever be used in the palace. *If only there were some way to make it more gripping, more dramatic . . .*

Josiah began singing the tune over and over in his mind, remembering all those details he had carefully blended together to give the tune order, unity, and balance. Building on what Kochesh had done he constructed an introduction that seized attention with sharp dissonance; instead of starting with the shout of love, he went directly to the first cry for help. With building disaccord, he imagined the floods of sorrow and the shaking earth. Josiah excitedly focused his mind as a stream of inspiration came. A great musical drama about the clash between Jehovah and the floods of sorrow unfolded. From the pits of sorrow Jehovah rescued him and lifted him, higher and higher, until finally He broke through the powerful chaos and filled the world with saving light!

The composer took a deep breath and reflected on his burst of creativity, strong emotions slowly fading away. Then he laughed at himself for getting so absorbed. But he liked what he had created.

Josiah walked with Casil toward the western gate as afternoon shadows crept across the road. The hottest part of the day was past, but the air was very still on the streets of Jerusalem. People moved about as the day drew to a close. Tomorrow would be the sixth day of the week when many urban Israelites worked only part of the day, reserving the afternoon and evening for family dinners, concerts, games, and other diversions. However, most Levites and other pious people would be at home by sundown in order to observe the Sabbath evening. Consequently tonight, the evening before the sixth day, was the night Levite schoolmates could stay out a little later than normal.

Ahead, the gate tower rose over two buildings that abutted the city wall, one a storehouse and the other a stable for the guards' horses. Some thirty people loitered and talked in the open area just inside the gate. Since he didn't see any of his friends yet, Josiah took a seat on a stone ledge and propped his harp beside him. Casil wandered over to a team of horses hitched outside the stables.

Josiah tried to imagine what this festival was going to be like. His school and family sometimes had big feasts together, especially on national holidays. But he had never heard of a festival just for people his age from all across the city.

He leaned the harp against his chest and started strumming a tune he had made up the year before. He sang softly with it, thinking of the lush gardens of the Kidron Valley on a summer afternoon. Several passersby smiled at him, appreciating the melody, but Josiah hardly noticed them. He didn't even see the tall figure of Shammoth until he was close enough to touch.

"Come to be our evening entertainment?" asked the guard as Josiah kept playing.

"I'm not appreciated up the hill, so I thought I'd try an easier audience."

Shammoth propped one foot on the ledge and examined the boy's harp. "Is that yours?" he asked.

"It's my gift for being a good student."

"What's it worth?" When Josiah told him, the thick eyebrows rose. "You must be a talented musician. Did your father teach you to play?"

"Music is not my dad's gift. He's the kind to slaughter small animals."

While Shammoth wondered what to say next, Casil walked up. He eyed the soldier for a moment before recognizing him. "So how is business? Arrested anyone today?"

"No one of consequence. Are you boys wasting time or did you come just to serenade us?"

"We're just meeting some friends," Casil answered.

"Some others are having a feast out in the country," Josiah added. Casil glanced at him meaningfully.

"You'll have a good evening for it when it cools off. Do I need to keep the gate open longer for you?"

Josiah had not really thought about the curfew, but he said, "If they go too late I'm leaving. Casil is the one who likes to stay out all night."

"Well, play us some music while you wait for your companions. Do you know any whirls?"

Josiah started into a familiar song on his harp. A whirl was the name for a common song that encouraged the hearers to clap their hands and whirl around in a happy dance. A flute or pipe usually led, so Josiah whistled its part over the harp's harmony. Casil supplied the beat by pounding his chest and thigh. Shammoth, another guard, and a few others joined in, slapping their thighs or whistling. One man got up and whirled out in the street until a passing chariot nearly ran over him. The others cheered and laughed as he shook himself and sat back down.

During the merriment Jedan walked up with Beriah following. Jedan had his pipe and was glad to play a round of the song. A small crowd had gathered in front of the gate by the time they finished. When they dispersed, Josiah saw two familiar faces approaching. Hannah and Rachel looked amused. "I thought the festival was outside the city!" Rachel said.

A city gate consisted of a series of room-sized chambers divided by stone walls set with heavy gates. Whenever there was a chance someone might be taking stolen goods out of the city or bringing contraband into it, guards in each room could stop a traveler and check his baggage. If the city were attacked, the chambers and gates provided a stout defense, requiring attackers to fight through every successive chamber. For any walled city, the entrances were by far the weakest points and had to have sturdy protection. Shammoth held a very important position as a chief guard, combining the responsibilities of a soldier, security guard, policeman, and customs official. The gates were open to free traffic that afternoon, so the six Levites took leave of Shammoth, left Jerusalem, and walked along the dusty road west.

Casil led, following the directions Kochesh gave him. Josiah looked toward the horizon where the sun would enter in a few hours. Two days' travel in that direction was Ashkelon, the old Philistine city Kochesh claimed as his home. Josiah had twice traveled to Joppa, an Israelite port farther north on the coast of the Great Sea. He had gone several times with his family to the north of the kingdom to visit their relatives and friends. But he had never been to a city that wasn't mostly Israelite. Everyone knew of the grandeur of the Philistines in former days, before King David defeated them. They had mastered ironwork, soaring architecture, and horsemanship. Much of Israel's technology had been gradually acquired from the Philistines.

"What's on your mind?" asked Hannah brightly. The others were talking and joking, feeling free because the week was coming to a close. School was such a light load on sixth day mornings that everyone felt lighthearted.

"Oh, nothing in particular," Josiah answered, inaccurately.

After a few more steps, Hannah spoke again. "What are you going to play tonight?"

"I'll see what sort of people we have listening. If it's a group of commoners, we'll stay with the common songs. If Kochesh brings a noble crowd, we can play the good songs."

"He seemed to have a lot of nice people and rich people around his shop. I think they'll like the best we can offer. You should play some of the praise tunes."

"Out here? That would *not* sound right." Josiah laughed at the thought. "Like Johanon always says, 'The music of worship is sacred to the service of Jehovah.'" He thickened his voice and whined a little in a decent imitation of his teacher's voice, earning a laugh from Hannah.

"But why not?" she asked. "Why can't we serve Jehovah out here? He's still God in all of Israel, isn't He? I don't see how our songs of praise can be good inside the palace of Jehovah but not outside of it." She paused. "Jehovah is supposed to be everywhere. If Jehovah is everywhere, He can hear music anywhere. If He likes the music we play in His palace, He should like the music we play everywhere else!"

"If places didn't matter, would Jehovah have a palace at all?" Josiah countered. "Do we offer sacrifices just anywhere we want? Do we burn incense just anywhere we want?" He looked at her, but it cost him his train of thought. After looking back to the west for a little, he continued. "Don't you do things at home you wouldn't do at school? Singing palace music outside of the palace seems to, well . . ." He trailed off.

"I see what you mean," said Hannah. "Still, as good as Kochesh is with music, he probably would enjoy some of the best songs. Maybe you could play the piece you wrote for the competition."

"Is it one of the best songs?" Josiah kidded, looking at her again.

"It's good," she replied, smiling. "I like it."

He looked down and laughed, pleased but self-conscious. He started to tell her about the changes he had made to the composition, but didn't. They walked on quietly until Rachel's voice sounded behind them. "Hey, how much farther, Casil?"

"Just over that ridge," was the answer. Casil walked well ahead of the others. After walking west some distance they had left the road, turning northwest into a small valley. The ridge Casil apparently meant was a low rise at the head of the valley. They had seen a small group of people cross the rise ahead of them. With the main road now out of sight, no one else was to be seen. The palace of Jehovah was barely visible in the distance.

They hiked up the ridge at an angle. As they reached its crest, a green field opened below them. It was too rocky for crops, but must have been a popular sheep pasture. At the far end of the field was a small hill in front of a half-circle of woods. They were apparently at the right place, for a crowd was gathered around the hill. Josiah's attention went immediately to the hilltop where about fifteen brightly robed figures sat or stood around a wooden pole. The pole was twice the height of a man, painted colorfully and decorated with flowers and greenery.

Happy music and the hum of conversation drifted to them as they approached. A young man noticed them, smiled, and raised his hand in greeting. Casil told him how they had learned about the festival. At the name of Kochesh, the man nodded and smiled again. He told them to make themselves comfortable on the grass and have some food while he let Kochesh know they had arrived.

Josiah looked around at the assembly. Groups ranging in size from five to fifty clustered about and below the hill, eating or talking. Most were young people, many of them school age. The man who had welcomed them was one of the older ones present. Josiah supposed him to be about ten years older than himself. Some of those present looked as young as twelve.

Three girls came around with baskets of dates and figs. Josiah and his friends took a handful each (Beriah filled both hands) and stretched themselves on the grass to eat. Through a mouthful of fruit, Jedan wondered aloud what the ornamented pole was for. "It's probably to show everyone where to come for the feast," commented Josiah. "Do you know, Casil?"

"I think they're going to have a circle later on. The pole probably marks the center." By a "circle" he meant a type of large group dance in which the participants formed two or more concentric circles that moved in opposite directions, occasionally darting between each other to switch the inner and outer circles. It was a beautifully intricate display when performed by a large and well-rehearsed group. Young people enjoyed circling because it was active and exciting, especially when the circles switched. Brief inattention could result in a collision, and one collision could cause a series of trips and falls. Boys in an informal circle sometimes made it a competition to see who could be the last standing.

None of them had seen Kochesh until he appeared striding down the slope of the hill. He wore a red cloak over a white robe trimmed in gold. His smile was bright, his shoulders square, and his bearing confident. He clasped arms with Casil and then each of them in turn, expressing his pleasure in their arrival. "Are you all ready to perform for us? I've told some of the others about you and your abilities. We are eager to hear your songs and share your feelings. I hope you will be completely comfortable, knowing that everyone here has come to have fun."

He walked off leaving the six friends to watch as a group of boys started a stone-throwing contest. They picked up rocks of various sizes and competed to see who could hurl them farthest down the field. Some girls were singing well-known songs about romance and happiness. Good smells came from a corner of the field in which someone was preparing the food. Josiah found himself getting drowsy. Just then, a man and woman he didn't know approached.

"Hello! You're musicians, aren't you? Good! The feast will be ready soon, but you can play for us before we eat." The man spoke with a Judean accent, but when the woman spoke she revealed a slight foreign accent. Her Hebrew was very precise, however.

"Bring your instruments up to the hill so everyone can hear you," she said. "Play us something lively."

Casil sprang up with his bow harp and jogged up the slope. Josiah and the others followed. As he tested the strings of his harp, Josiah looked out from the hill over the crowd in wonder. There were hundreds of young people dressed in a brilliant rainbow of colors. A few looked up at him expectantly, having noticed that a new group of musicians was about to play. Casil called the name of a familiar tune and struck its first chord. The others came in smartly. A hush washed over the crowd below as the music burst forth.

Beriah transitioned the group from one tune to the next with his trumpet. They played on for some time, with the listeners apparently enjoying themselves.

It was time to eat. Josiah resumed his place on the grass in the field and set his harp down beside him. Other musicians took turns playing gentle music as they ate a delicious meal. After finishing, Josiah and his friends stretched out to relax and enjoy the cool air until Kochesh approached again.

"Here, Levites! Let's have you play for everyone again. Get them in the mood to enjoy our show later. Perhaps Josiah can play us that mighty psalm."

The group took their instruments up again. Casil first led them in a song about harvest time celebration, featuring Beriah's powerful solo voice. Then Casil signaled Josiah to lead them in his psalm composition.

Josiah called to his mind the flow of music he had generated earlier. His hands settled on the strings of his harp but remained motionless. The tune played through his imagination while his detached conscience criticized it. *Is this good music? Will they like it? Should I change something?* His chest tightened as he imagined the emotional crisis of the rescue. Then the pure joy of victory welled inside, and he wanted so much to convey it to everyone in the land.

But this psalm is so long.

Josiah leaned back. "Hey, something wrong?" whispered Casil. They all looked at him. Everyone was looking at him.

"No." Josiah made a decision and drew his hand across the harp.

> They encompassed me, the cords of death!
> And the rivers of wickedness terrified me!

Everyone's attention was riveted on Josiah as he plunged into the song. With gripping tension he carried it through the cries for help. The shaking of the earth became a setting for conflict between order and chaos. Then Josiah did something unusual for a Levite musician; he omitted the next eight verses.

> He sent from the heights—He took me!
> He drew me out of many waters.

Josiah sang on about the rescue of the psalmist by Jehovah. The other musicians followed him with their instruments, making a joyous sound.

> He brought me out into a broad place,
> He rescued me because He delighted in me!

Thus he ended the praise stanza triumphantly. Immediately he went on with a rich melody, but skipped other verses to sing the ones he wanted.

> Jehovah rewarded me according to my righteousness,
> According to the cleanness of my hands He recompensed me.
> I was perfect with Him,
> And I kept myself from iniquity;

So Jehovah rewarded me according to my righteousness
According to the cleanness of my hands before his eyes.

With the faithful you will be faithful,
With the perfect you will be perfect.
For by you I can run against a troop,
By my God I can leap over a wall!

Josiah then reverted to the three verses at the beginning of the psalm that he had skipped initially. He brought the music to a climax and sang with all his voice:

> I will love thee, Jehovah, my strength!
> Jehovah, my rock, my fortress, my deliverer,
> My God, my mountain, I take refuge in Him.
> My shield, and the horn of my salvation, my stronghold.
> I will call on Jehovah—Be praised!
> And from my enemies I will be saved!

As the melody descended the scale, he ended with a brilliant resolution. The field was silent a moment, then the great group lifted up an appreciative cheer. Josiah was startled; it was the first time a large number of people had actually applauded his singing. Whenever he played or sang in a palace service, no one cheered. Josiah felt carried away to have so many praise him at once.

"Very good, mighty man!" Kochesh smiled as broadly as ever, slapping his thigh as he approached. "A marvelous way to move the mind and heart. They love you! Go enjoy a rest while we entertain you."

The six newly famous musicians descended from the hill back to their place on the grass and sat down to watch. Josiah looked up into a beautiful orange and yellow sky. The sun was low but still bright. "That was great," whispered Hannah's voice in his ear. "But why did you leave out so much? You should have played it all. It would have been even better." He looked at her and thought about a reply, but the play was starting. He just smiled at her for a moment and then looked away.

On top of the hill, Kochesh and his assistants began a curious presentation. Four of them had put on colorful costumes to signify their parts in a theatric. Eight others stood in a semicircle at the back, apparently a chorus. Kochesh himself stood to one side, *probably to sing a solo,* Josiah thought.

Some instrumentalists off the hill began a cheerful melody. One actor, cloaked in silver and gold, raised one arm and walked with dignity around the crest of the hill.

> Lord Dagon, Giver of rain and harvest,
> To you will we give praise with heart and voice.

The chorus chanted in harmony. A girl dressed in green and purple and draped with various flowers danced festively around the lordly Dagon, who surveyed the field with satisfaction.

The music changed to an ominous theme. *There must be an evil character coming,* Josiah supposed. Sure enough, a third figure in black robes swept onto the scene. He crept up behind Dagon and seized him. The two wrestled briefly as the music throbbed. Black won, subdued Dagon, and dragged him away.

> Death, son of darkness, master of deaths!
> Will you raise your hand against the lord of heaven?

Flower Girl came looking for her lord. Not finding him, she broke into sobbing while the music played a dirge and the chorus went on at length about Death and his pernicious ways.

The dirge came to a rest. The chorus began a soft song about the cold of winter, the lack of rain, and the absence of crops. Their enemies were threatening, many people were sick, and no children were being born.

They sounded so sad Josiah felt his eyes moisten. He glanced at Hannah; she was nearly in tears. *Some festival,* he thought. The clear, strong voice of Kochesh sounded.

> Who can break the chains of Death,
> Bring light and fire to our winter?
> Our lord lies prisoner of hated Death,
> Death the robber of fruit.

Time for a hero theme, Josiah predicted. But Kochesh wasn't finished with his song.

> Great Lord Dagon we recall your goodness
> Bestowed daily in the waters of life.
> What sacrifice will buy you life?

> Queen Asherah, daughter of gods
> In longing to you we pray,
> We ask you to become his savior,
> And our savior, Mother, Queen, O Asherah.

Now came the hero theme. Josiah watched and listened as a woman clothed in bright scarlet swept onto the scene. Asherah, no doubt. She held a silver rod. Asherah ran to her left and down the back of the hill. At the same time Death and Dagon came to the forefront, Dagon acting bound and weak, Death gloating over him. Asherah emerged behind them. The music was tense, rattling. Suddenly she lunged and struck Death's head with her rod. She tried to drag the staggering Dagon away. Death drew a dagger and charged them, but a second blow from the wand put him on his knees. Asherah and Dagon escaped.

As the heroine and her rescued lord "emerged" onto the hill again, the chorus sang for joy at the return of warmth and life to the land. Crops grew, rain fell, birds sang. Flower Girl flitted about merrily. Dagon and Asherah marched serenely around the crown of the hill while Kochesh sang praise to their glorious, eternal reign.

The sprawling field of young people cheered the performers as the theatric closed. "What was that all about?" Josiah asked Casil.

"Death captures the lord, and Asherah goes down to the underworld and rescues him. It's an old Canaanite story. I'm sure Kochesh can tell us all about it."

Kochesh came around to them some time later. The drama, as he explained, was their way of entertainingly retelling a familiar story. Dagon, son and servant to the great god, gives rain and fertility to the land and people. Death takes him in an attempt to destroy or enslave the entire world. But Asherah bravely rescues her lord and husband from Death, returns him to heaven, and restores him to his rightful rule over the earth. He then brings fruitfulness back to those who worship him.

"It's the same beautiful story of death, sorrow, courage, and new birth common to all faiths," finished Kochesh.

"But not to the ways of Israel," corrected Hannah.

"Yes, even for Israel," Kochesh responded with a friendly laugh. "You confess the great God, as we all do. You call the lord who rules earth Jehovah; the Philistines call him Dagon. We all put on different outer garments, but all are the same stuff of man underneath." Kochesh laid his arm on Josiah's shoulders. "Come up to the hill with me. Bring that lovely harp." Josiah smirked at what Casil must be thinking.

Back on the hill in full view of the lounging assembly Kochesh and Josiah sat side by side. "Look at how peaceful and happy they all are," Kochesh said to Josiah. "Meat feeds their stomachs; music feeds their hearts. You've helped give them a delightful evening."

"It was fun," Josiah acknowledged.

"Would anything make it even better for them?" He drew Josiah's attention to a trio of boys. "What would they like?"

"No school at all tomorrow so they could stay up past bedtime." *Playing games, stretching out on a roof to count stars and talk, sneak into the larder in the middle of the night to get some honey cakes,* Josiah continued to himself.

"How about them?" This time Kochesh pointed to two young women leaning close together, whispering.

"Probably a room where no one can hear them so they can gossip all night."

"Yes. They all want the pleasure of each other's company, putting off the labor of tomorrow to savor the present moment. Like those two under the sycamore." A boy and girl around Josiah's age sat together at the edge of the field, out of the main group. Josiah chuckled and agreed.

"And what companion would you choose? Casil and the other fellows? Or a young lady?"

Josiah thought that question silly. "Casil's entertaining, I suppose, but I envy the fellow under the tree. Or I would, if I had a wife."

"You like the young lady, Hannah?"

"Sure." Josiah was a little uncomfortable and tried to sound nonchalant.

"Yes, everyone enjoys companionship, especially that between a man and woman. You know, Josiah, you can give these friends something of what would make their evening most complete. You have a wonderful gift. Your powers of music can dispel thoughts of tomorrow and let them delight in this moment." Kochesh took Josiah's harp and began a soft, soothing melody.

At first, it was unremarkable. But ever so easily it changed. Josiah heard the harp play a sound he had not heard before. Thick harmonics filled his mind. Other instruments softly joined—the other musician friends of Kochesh. The tune wandered nimbly, engagingly, never quite forming a melody, irregularly repeating certain patterns. It was very pleasant, but strange to Josiah's ear.

Kochesh changed again to a more familiar form, but the tune was not familiar. Josiah was awed by it. He closed his eyes at the beauty it held, feeling his emotion well up inside.

"What would you tell her, Josiah?" The question made no sense. "What would you tell her if you could open your heart freely, with no one to judge you for it? Here, say it." Kochesh handed Josiah the harp, black under the vanishing sun.

"What do you mean?"

"You know," Kochesh whispered assuredly. "Imagine the harp is your only voice and you have only this once to tell her how you feel."

The little band still played a mellow rhythm. Josiah joined them as a burst of creativity came from within. He heard, then played the sentimental song, speaking warmth, tenderness, love, and trust.

"Look at them now," Kochesh urged after a while. Everywhere Josiah looked he saw a young couple sitting close, drinking in the music. He thought of Hannah, and imagined himself speaking to her. He played on.

When Josiah's instrument fell silent, the sun was out of sight, leaving a red sky behind. Josiah inhaled deeply, and relaxed, causing a disaster. His harp fell from his arm and struck a sharp rock, gashing it and snapping one string. He snatched it up and inspected the damage. *Johanon will not be pleased,* he groaned inwardly. He was relieved to see that no one else had noticed.

Kochesh stood and addressed the festival participants. "Thank you all for coming and sharing your evening with us. I trust everyone enjoyed the feast. But the sun soon goes in, and so must all of us. Be sure to get inside the gate before it is closed, so Father and Mother won't worry. Farewell!"

As the kids rose and stretched, most were clearly reluctant to leave, but they began heading back toward the main road in twos and threes. Kochesh addressed Josiah and his friends one last time. "You fine music makers should come with me on a visit to Ashkelon next month. You would all profit greatly from hearing great minstrels from around the world. I'll be gone two weeks to collect new merchandise, and would love to have you along. You can stay with my family and friends. Would you like that?"

"Yes!" Casil answered quickly. The others agreed it sounded great, and would think about it. Josiah answered nothing, but his mind's eye pictured the sights and sounds of Ashkelon. "I'm sure it is a wonderful place," he told Kochesh.

Notes to the Reader

Canaanite Religion

Archaeologists have learned that the religion of Canaan, the land into which God sent the children of Israel, was extremely wicked and debauched. The ancient city of **Ugarit** was north of Israel on the coast of the Mediterranean Sea in what is now Syria. Excavations at Ugarit have turned up thousands of written tablets that include the stories used to express what its people believed about their gods. Beliefs throughout Canaan (which encompassed all the land that is now Syria, Lebanon, Israel, and Jordan) were similar. Therefore, the finds at Ugarit reveal the basic features of the false religion that God's people Israel were in constant danger of adopting.

Canaanite worship centered on farming. Harvesting crops was the most important part of their lives, since one failed crop could mean starvation. Religion, therefore, was not a matter of morals or ethics—it wasn't for teaching behavior; rather, it was a way of getting the gods to do what one wanted. All religions besides that revealed by God in the Bible are invented by man and serve man's purposes instead of God's. The Canaanite religion did exactly that.

The most important god of many was called "the Baal." *Baal* means lord or boss. Though it is not a proper name, it can be used like one, just as the English word *god* can mean any false god or can be used as a name for the one true God. The actual name of the Baal varied from region to region because each region in Canaan had a different god it considered its own. Consequently, the Baal in Ugarit was named Hadad ("Baal-Hadad"); the Baal in Moab was named Chemosh ("Baal-Chemosh"); the Baal in Philistia, who appears in the theatric at the youth festival, was named Dagon ("Baal-Dagon"). First Samuel 5:1-2 records a time when the Philistines captured the ark of Jehovah in battle and put it in the palace of Dagon in the city of Ashdod.

Wherever he appeared and under whatever name, Baal was the god of lightning and rain. He was vital to farming because he supposedly sent the rain. The stories found at Ugarit show that the Canaanites explained times when rainfall was short by saying that Baal was gone from home. Only when he was home could he send rain. His chief reason for leaving home was to fight the god Muth, whose name is the word for death. He was death personified, and so his name is "Death" in the story you are reading.

Death always defeated Dagon when Dagon came to fight him. A goddess named Asherah (sometimes Anath), who appeared sometimes as Dagon's wife and sometimes as his sister, was the only one who could rescue the god from Death. When she brought him back home, he sent rain to earth again.

Baal worship all over Canaan was characterized by flagrant immorality. At times human sacrifice occurred, especially the sacrifice of children. Considering how selfish, greedy, and vile their made-up gods were, it is no wonder the people saw nothing wrong with such wickedness in their own lives.

Review and Discussion

1. What kind of relationship does Josiah seem to have with his parents?

2. Do you think the teacher Johanon would find anything wrong with the "whirl" Josiah and the others play for people while waiting at the Western Gate?

3. For what reasons does Josiah not like Hannah's suggestion that they play the best psalm tunes at the festival? Does he later do what she suggested when he plays at the festival?

4. Why do you suppose Kochesh wanted Josiah and his friends to play for the crowd at the festival?

5. What does Kochesh intend by having Josiah "speak" with his harp at the end of the festival?

CHAPTER FOUR

Halfway

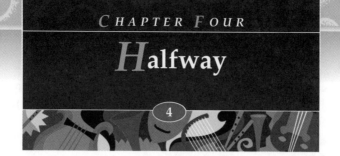

"Dad, have you ever been to Ashkelon?"

Adaiah kept sharpening his knife and didn't respond to the abrupt question. They had been talking about what to have for supper. Josiah was routinely copying a scroll of the fifth book of Moses, *These Are the Words,* an assignment from Johanon.

"The Philistine city on the coast," Josiah added.

"No. Why?"

Josiah looked down at his scroll while he gathered his thoughts. "Do you know anything about it? Would I like to visit there?"

"I don't know why. I've heard it has pretty buildings, but it's just a Philistine merchandise market, full of their filth. I once talked with a Levite who lives there. He went there to teach a little group of Israelites and hoped to get a chance to teach some foreigners to serve Jehovah. Most of them think we are little children to have only one God, he told me."

"What are the Philistines like?"

"Like all the nations: selfish, debauched, hating Jehovah. Why?"

"Some Israelites are selfish and debauched. Even some Levites are." There was a short silence. "I met a man who thinks I would like to visit Ashkelon. He says, . . . says the city can teach me about other peoples like the Egyptians and Grecians. Like Joppa."

"Who is this?" Adaiah looked up from his knife.

Josiah answered carefully. "A shopkeeper down in the foreigners' bazaar. He sells good things from all around the world and is making a trip to the west to buy some stuff. He's very skilled at music and invited me to come with him. Casil, too."

"How have you and Casil come to know this man?"

"Casil met him in the market and took us to meet him. Jedan and Beriah went too. They know him too."

"Joppa is an Israelite city. Ashkelon is Philistine. They won't break the law of the king openly, but there are dangerous sons of Belial there. Why did you say he wants you to visit that place? How long would you be gone?"

"Only a week. He wants me to see the great musicians there from other lands. I could learn a lot about music in just a couple of days."

Adaiah returned to sharpening his knife and said nothing more. Josiah resented his father's suspicion. *He thinks I'm still a child who can't go far from home.*

"What was so bad about the Philistines? Were they so much worse than other nations?"

"Yes," Adaiah returned, then hesitated. "They were not worse than other foreigners. But they *were* worse because they afflicted and oppressed us more and longer than any other foreigners."

"But they haven't oppressed us for a long time, not even since you were born. True?"

"True—not that that was so long ago. But my father was in the last wars they fought, when King David beat them for the last time."

"But haven't we taken a lot of good things from them? We learned about iron, horses and chariots, and architecture from them. Didn't King Solomon marry a Philistine woman?"

"King Solomon marries foreign women to keep peace and to show his political superiority. And yes, we learned some things from the foreigners, but those are not what made them such an evil, debauched people."

"Then what did?" Josiah asked, his voice rising a little.

Adaiah sat back and put his knife down. His brow furrowed as he worked on an explanation. "Jehovah gave us this land because He promised He would, but the people who lived here were very evil. They had to be destroyed. Jehovah endured them a long time, and gave them plenty of chances to repent, but they never did. So He had Joshua destroy them."

"What about the Philistines? Joshua didn't destroy the Philistines."

"The Philistines weren't in our land in Joshua's day. Jehovah used them to chastise our people when they sinned, a long time after Joshua."

"Then if Jehovah made them our enemies, why do we think of them as being so evil? Weren't *we* the evil ones?"

"Because they *were* evil!" Adaiah showed his frustration and fell silent. Josiah continued copying.

Taking a breath, Adaiah continued. "Son, you know a lot. You've learned so much from the master Levites and the priests. Ask one of them—ask Master Johanon about the Philistines. They and the other Canaanites did horrible acts in the worship of their vile gods."

"How many Philistines have you known?" Josiah asked his father.

"I've met several." Adaiah resumed sharpening his knife and didn't elaborate.

"What if you met a Philistine who worshiped Jehovah?"

"I would rejoice with him and give thanks to our great God for having mercy on the son of an evil nation."

"Could he still be a Philistine and worship Jehovah?"

"A Philistine by blood, but he must become a son of Israel in his heart. The life of Philistia, its wicked pleasures and filthy gods, he must abandon." Adaiah looked up as a thought came to him. "This merchant friend who wants to take you to Ashkelon, is he a Philistine?"

Josiah paused momentarily. "N-no," he said. "And anyway, how can we say someone has to leave everything he used to be to follow Jehovah? The king's wives sacrifice to the gods of their nations even though they live beside the palace of Jehovah."

Adaiah looked up sharply. "The king's wives are not daughters of Israel. Not all of them, at least. And those that worship other gods cannot worship Jehovah, for He says, 'You shall have no other gods before me.' "

"But what if Jehovah gets first place? Or what if a Philistine doesn't really believe his old religion but still likes to see the value in it?"

"*What* value? Josiah, the Philistines and all Canaanites serve filthy gods of wood and stone that demand horrible sacrifices and cause the most awful sins and call it worship!"

"I'm sorry, Dad; I was just asking a question." Josiah decided not to pursue the issue farther. His dad had not said yes, but he hadn't said no, either.

Josiah loved the sound of the Levites' singing. Four hundred men harmonized one of Asaph's psalms. Their chords rolled over the palace wall and through the stone streets.

After entering the open gate, Josiah found a Levite porter and asked if he knew where Master Johanon was. Informed that his teacher had walked down toward the Forest palace not long ago, Josiah headed after him. A shuffling ruckus drew his attention. A large family had entered through the north gate and was walking along the wall to the front of Jehovah's palace. They were clearly not city people. They led several goats and lambs. The lambs were as perfectly white as Josiah had ever seen. A child, perhaps eight years old, led one, stroking its neck.

Josiah's stomach tightened. He turned away, feeling pain and anger; that little girl was about to see her pet slaughtered by her own father. He glanced at the blank back wall of the palace of Jehovah, towering up from the crest of the hill. He imagined God sitting inside, listening to the sound of a little girl's crying as her father cut the lamb's throat.

Josiah walked quickly toward the south wall. Another gate opened into the peaceful grounds of Solomon's palaces. Soldiers, servants, and a few royal officials were to be seen going about their afternoon business. The ornate building directly ahead was his destination.

The palace of the Forest of Lebanon was strikingly beautiful. In its polished stone wall were set three rows of windows. An ornate entrance ushered one into its cool interior. Josiah wouldn't have been there without a good reason; the structure served a variety of functions and was normally off limits to students. But he had been inside a few times before and welcomed another chance.

Lebanon was the source of the fine, aromatic cedar wood prized for use in construction. This palace was so named because it was filled with great cedar pillars, each a single tree trunk, running all the way to the cedar roof three stories over Josiah's head. The square windows faced each other from either long wall in the oblong building. They flooded its interior with yellow sunlight but kept out heat. Ivy, ferns, and flowers decorated the "forest" with greenery and added a palette of smells to go with the pungent cedar.

A network of small walkways, stairways, and platforms at different heights linked the cedar pillars and the walls, creating the illusion of a thousand branches filling the air, patterned, but asymmetric, like a real forest. Visitors and royal officers resting in the palace could walk among the three different levels, sit against the trunk of a tree high above the floor, or look out a window onto the palace grounds and surrounding countryside. No solid walls partitioned the palace's interior, but the maze of pathways and the quiet ensured by so much open space allowed private conversations to go on almost anywhere inside.

The most awe-inspiring feature of the palace was its collection of glittering gold vessels displayed across all four walls. Most were for the service of the palace of Jehovah. They were kept stored in the Forest palace in dazzling display.

Many people bustled around the palace. Their robes made the scene even more colorful. However, the large number of white-clad priests and Levites among them made it difficult for Josiah to pick out the one he sought. Finally, he saw his teacher reclining at the base of one pillar; Johanon was engaging a priest in conversation. Josiah never liked interrupting older men, but he felt too conspicuous to wait around. He caught Johanon's eye and bowed low. "Master Johanon, I have not received my harp. Would it be possible to have it back soon?"

"Ah, yes, your trip next week. You will practice every day, I trust? And not damage your gift a second time?" Josiah's cheeks felt warm, especially due to the presence of the bearded priest, who studiously ignored him. He mumbled a promise to be more careful.

To Josiah's surprise, Johanon turned back to the priest and excused himself. He then arose and motioned for Josiah to follow. It had been necessary to get the master's permission to recover the harp from its mender, but he could have retrieved it without Johanon's presence. Josiah wondered what the old man was going to do.

The two of them walked out of the Forest palace and back across the grounds of the palace of Jehovah. More families were gathered to offer personal sacrifices. Josiah saw the same family he had seen earlier. No animals accompanied them now, but they bore three bundles that Josiah knew to be their portion of meat. As he had expected, the little girl was softly crying.

When Johanon turned toward them, Josiah stayed back, wondering what his teacher had to say to a simple farm family. The father was smiling as he bowed to Master Johanon. Somehow that angered Josiah.

"Greeting, Micaiah!" began Johanon. "Is all well with you?"

"Greeting, Teacher! Jehovah is so good to me and to my family. We have brought today burnt offerings and freewill offerings to His palace. Is all well with you?" The farmer had an honest face and a country dialect. He obviously knew Johanon. They exchanged news on family and friends. When the farmer mentioned his youngest daughter, Johanon looked at the little girl and motioned her to come to him. She obeyed. The Levite knelt down to look her in the face, a face still reddened and moist from tears.

"My dear one, why do you cry?" Johanon asked tenderly. She whispered something Josiah could not hear. "Jehovah our God cries with you. He knows it hurts. But it hurts Him when we break His Law. If you love and trust Jehovah, one day no more lambs will have to die." Johanon embraced her gently and let her go back to her mother. He stood and clasped hands with Micaiah, and after some parting words continued out the gate with a glance at Josiah.

Josiah caught up with his teacher and asked who they were. "Farmers of Judah, from west of Bethlehem where I ministered for some years before returning to teach young men of the privileged class—those who don't associate with farmers. You might have come up to make their acquaintance. I assure you they are disease-free." Josiah was stung. He muttered an apology and looked away.

They reached the covered porch of a building when Johanon stopped and faced his student. "I don't mean to be harsh. But common people are very important. They are the flock we shepherd and the vineyard we tend. Being set aside by Jehovah to be their teachers does not mean we deserve more than they."

"Master Johanon, I don't think that! I thought he—" Not wanting to say, *I thought he was trying to impress you with his piety while ignoring his child,* Josiah broke off.

"Micaiah is as kindhearted a man as I know. He teaches his children well. Though it is very painful to the little one, it is the best way to teach her the awful pain caused by sin. She hardly understands what happens in the world around her, but she understands that another, an innocent, must suffer because she or a member of her family sins."

Josiah stood still for a moment, then asked if he could have his harp. Wordlessly Johanon led the way inside to his own private chamber instead of the craft hall. There on the floor was Josiah's beautiful black harp, perfectly mended. He took it up and struck a chord to test its tune. With minor adjustment it sounded just right. Josiah thanked his teacher and bowed in departure, but Johanon spoke. "Are you prepared for the composition contest?"

"Almost, Master Johanon. I will practice next week."

"The music of a Levite is very important, and you have an unusual gift for robing our message in new song. Your shepherding with song is as vital as any ministry of the priests and Levites. But you must understand sacrifice if you will teach others the truth."

"I do understand, Master Johanon. But I don't like it, and don't see why I should. Isn't it supposed to be a horrible thing, only a result of sin?"

"When was the last time you offered a freewill offering?"

"My father offers those for our family."

"Your father offers them in gratitude for his family, but from himself. Each man must lift up his own freewill offering. No sin calls them forth." Josiah knew that and waited to see if his teacher had finished. He hadn't. "When was the last time you sang a song of praise to Jehovah alone, with no one around to hear but Him? You asked no blessing, made no request, only sang to Him in joy." Josiah wasn't sure what response was expected, so he kept quiet. He sang songs to himself every day. Johanon, however, probably just wanted to give whatever advice was on his mind before letting him go. "Your song is like a freewill offering; you take your time and strength to give Jehovah a sign that you love Him."

"And prophesy to others of His greatness and goodness," completed Josiah to show that he understood.

"Can a man prophesy to others what he does not himself believe?" asked Johanon.

Josiah considered. "I don't know," he answered honestly.

"Can you, Josiah, son of Adaiah, really make others feel the power of a song unless you feel it first?"

"Yes. I can play a song without thinking about it."

"But do the hearers feel it when you try that? Do they get the weight of the music if you don't pour it out of your own heart?"

Obviously no was the expected answer, but Josiah was unsure what to say. Fortunately his teacher continued. "If Jehovah has set you apart to teach others about Himself through music, you must know Him first. Your own life must be blameless before His Law. You must not sing His songs to the people while showing them you have no fear of or love for Him." Johanon sat down on his couch in a manner that told Josiah the lesson was ending. "I hope this trip of yours is a blessing. Wherever you are going, find an opportunity to sing a song to Jehovah. A song from yourself."

The market was busier than normal. Early evening was a popular time to walk about the bazaars and plazas of the city. Josiah wore a light red robe instead of his Levite attire as he ambled around the Block and through the congested alley.

With no reason to hurry, he went left instead of straight to avoid the noisy crowd at the food bazaar. He was between the two main rows of Israelite merchants' houses. Some were old, formed of uncut stones stacked and roughly mortared together. Others were built of the cut and smoothed blocks used by all modern builders. King Solomon wanted the whole city rebuilt with such architecture before his death, but there was a long way to go, and many in Jerusalem liked the nostalgia of the great cobblestone walls. But the cut stone allowed buildings to grow two and three times as high. In rich, competitive Jerusalem, a new look and more comfortable space could mean the difference between commonality and fabulous wealth.

The clothing bazaar looked as busy as the food bazaar, so Josiah drifted toward the outer row of houses. He passed the carpenters' bazaar, a trio of open-ended structures displaying every type of furniture. Music wafted out of the inner courtyard of each as the woodworkers sought to provide a pleasant atmosphere that would relax people into spending more money.

Ahead was a gaudily decorated establishment dedicated to the merchandise of unusual animals. Josiah liked it there. He decided to see what was new before cutting across the middle of the market to Kochesh's shop.

One cluster of people in front of the building looked tense. Josiah found two short people and looked between them. A man sitting on the ground played a reed pipe. In front of him a cobra rose gracefully into the air.

"Will it bite him?" a little girl asked her father.

"It's not real," a boy whispered. "Yes it is!" retorted his friend. "Look at its tongue flick." The man steadily played on, while the snake calmly watched him, moving little. "Why doesn't it bite him?" a woman wondered. "Snakes like a good tune," her husband answered. The piper softened his tune and lulled the cobra softly back down into the clay basin from which it had risen.

The man grinned. "No snake can resist good music. Now I have another tune, one meant to lull snakes into giving money to poor, hungry performers. Just please make sure all coins fall into the *empty* pot." He slapped a lid over his snake, picked up another flat bowl and played a singsong melody one-handed while holding out the bowl for donations. Josiah slipped away, content to let others express appreciation.

He walked inside the house and noticed another scene. The interior courtyard was ringed with open stalls. All sorts of strange creatures were on display. Gruff animal sounds caught his ear. A furry black shape danced and wobbled excitedly in one stall. Josiah watched as a trainer cajoled it into playing with toys and performing tricks. "Serenade us!" the trainer ordered, and whistled. The manlike beast—called an ape, Josiah knew—started beating on a pair of barrel-sized drums. "Sing!" Another whistle. The ape hooted. Spectators laughed and teased. "How melodious!" one yelled. "He sings better than some men!" another joked. Josiah laughed with them for a while. The ape could do all sorts of acts. Then it seemed to get tired. When it was slow to obey, its trainer cracked his whip in the air, spurring the ape to more entertainment. Josiah finally felt bored, and left.

The southern outer row of the market was home to the animal traders. Other than the one house of prized exotic creatures, the row consisted of smelly exchanges for inglorious horses, cattle, camels, donkeys, sheep, and goats. At the row's end was the tanners' bazaar. Josiah elected a diagonal route across the market center.

A maze of alleys among tall, narrow buildings was the clothing bazaar. Dozens of traders in the houses and along the streets outside offered garments of all descriptions. Josiah's eye fell on a display of bright red silk robes. The seller spotted him. "Try one on! Highest quality silk, purest red dye, never fades. Makes you look like a mighty man!" Josiah smiled at the man but didn't stop to barter. He didn't have much money. Of course, the robe had been very attractive; it had the same cut and luster as the robes Kochesh wore.

He passed into the interior court of the market. He wove through the clusters of people standing or squatting in the open plaza. A roar of water and steam to his left turned his head. There at the end of an iron forge, a smith had dunked something into his cooling trough. He raised it with tongs. As the steam cleared, the object revealed was a sword blade. Extra long, it glowed with red fire. A group of boys watched the smith, showing the fascination and excitement Josiah felt. The smith admonished the boys to be careful; red iron will burn you, he warned.

Continuing from the forge, Josiah skirted the edge of the water drain in the court's center and saw the public address platform where he and Casil had crossed swords a few weeks ago, the first time he met Kochesh. He walked over to it instead of going directly to Kochesh's shop. The platform was unoccupied. People sat with their backs against it, eating and chattering. His fight with Casil played through his mind as he began singing softly to himself an old army chorus. It was replaced by the chant of Kochesh and his audience that he remembered from that day.

> Who is the man with a strong hand,
> The man who can swing an iron sword?

Maybe Casil won then, but I'll get him someday. He imagined the look on Casil's face when he took a sword thrust right in the center of his chest armor.

Josiah turned to leave and found himself looking into the entrance of one of the richest houses in the market, the house of Jewels. The house in which Kochesh kept his shop lay straight through it. So Josiah walked right in.

He was surrounded by sparkling stones set in belts, bracelets, neck chains, and earrings. There was a display of fine necklaces. His hand ran over each until he saw the perfect one. *Hannah would look beautiful in that one!* Lifting it, he examined the golden strand down to the red gem in its pendant. "An eye for quality!" The vendor smiled at him. "Is there some beautiful lady who would enjoy that?"

Josiah flushed. "I'll come back with money sometime."

"Only a hundred shekels and it's all hers." Josiah nodded and went his way. *I should get that for Hannah before I leave to make her think about me. I can probably talk him down to eighty-five or ninety, but where will I get that much and when will I come back to buy it?* He briefly envied regular boys, those who learned a trade and could earn a little money of their own. Josiah had walked through the house of Gilding and now stood in front of the Garnet, the house for foreign merchants from which Kochesh sold his goods.

Inside, Kochesh mingled with customers. Josiah recognized the man whom he had seen at the festival accompanying the woman with the foreign accent. He wandered around looking at the exotic wares until the shop had cleared. Kochesh appeared beside him.

"Greeting, mighty man! Are you prepared for our journey?"

"Yes. Hey, do I need money for any reason?"

"One always needs money, Josiah; it is the blood of the world." He showed mock horror at the question, then returned to his usual jollity. "Fear not poverty for another week, my young man. I can get you anything you need. In fact, I can get you anything. I want you to enjoy next week so much that Jerusalem seems to just fade away."

The man from the festival approached with a smile. "Is this Josiah the minstrel?"

"Even so. Josiah, this is Dagathan, husband to my sister." Josiah bowed to Dagathan.

"Have you told him the happy news?" asked Dagathan.

"No! Josiah, what would make this excursion perfect for you?"

"Not having to come back?"

Kochesh laughed heartily. "Just in terms of next week, what would make it ideal for you? Come up to my room and tell me if I have guessed correctly." Asking Dagathan to extinguish the lamps and close the door to his shop, Kochesh led Josiah through the back doorway onto the second floor balcony overlooking the inner courtyard of the Garnet. Josiah had not seen it before, and he was amazed. Wood and stone statuary lined the yard. Well-groomed trees divided the lawn in a neat pattern. And in the center was a small mound with a decorated pillar like the one Josiah had seen at the festival, only more elaborately decorated. The architecture of the Garnet was unique to Josiah, very foreign but very pleasing.

Kochesh led Josiah up a flight of stairs to the third floor and into an apartment directly over his shop. Josiah knew that many merchants of the marketplace lived in the same buildings they worked in, and Kochesh appeared to be no exception. Entering, he looked around on Kochesh's elegant hospitality room.

Hannah was there.

And Rachel, and the woman with the foreign accent they had met at the festival. The woman said, "You must be Josiah! I am Tashni, wife of Dagathan." Josiah bowed, and then just smiled at Hannah.

"As I told you, I can get you anything." Kochesh grinned triumphantly. Hannah was smiling very brightly. "I'm going too! And so is Rachel."

"Oh," said Josiah.

"Hannah's father is a most delightful man. I have had the pleasure of making his friendship these two weeks. He most graciously agreed that the trip would be a great benefit to her. Knowing that you and Rachel and other respectable Israelite merchants were part of our company, he graciously agreed to let her come. You may talk it up all you like after we are on our way. It's late now, and Tashni promised to have Hannah and Rachel home before the sun's entering. Come on, Josiah, let's have a look at something before you go." With that Kochesh put his arm around Josiah and steered him out the door as Hannah called a farewell to him.

"I can't believe Nahath is letting her go without going with her," Josiah remarked.

"It shows the blessed new age of trust between our peoples. Look at this." Kochesh had led them into a storeroom down one side of the third floor. He lifted a graceful musical instrument up to the light of the setting sun. It was a lyre of high quality. "I wanted to show you this before we left. It is worth as much as that harp of yours. I hope to find two or three more like it next week."

"It is really beautiful," Josiah agreed as he took the lyre and examined it.

"Enough; you need to get home to begin the Sabbath Day, and I've kept you long enough. I will see you at the caravansary at the going forth of the sun, first day of next week." He replaced the lyre and steered Josiah out the door and toward the stairs. "Remember to bring that lovely harp to show to my friends. And bring your sword; you never know what adventure we'll encounter on our way." He laughed merrily as he waved Josiah away.

The Sabbath Day had passed peacefully. Laubi had to worry over every detail of Josiah's packing; his brother and sister had to keep asking questions. They had traveled around Israel before, but never to Ashkelon or any other city of Philistia. Josiah felt compelled to embellish his answers, not wanting to disappoint them with just how little he knew.

His father asked questions too. He was as surprised as Josiah to hear that Nahath was allowing Hannah to go, but it seemed to reassure him. Josiah told him about the respectable Israelite merchants traveling with them—although he hadn't heard that until two days ago. Anyway, they would only be in Ashkelon two days of six, since it was a two-day journey one way. Josiah, Casil, Hannah, and Rachel would be home for the next Sabbath.

Josiah's pack weighed him down as he reached the Western Gate. Shammoth stopped him to find out why he was heading out of the city in travel clothes with a sack full of goods and a harp. Hannah and Rachel had just gone through, said Shammoth, their bags carried by a stranger. Shammoth acted very interested and remarked that he had heard of Kochesh.

After satisfying the guard, Josiah trudged down the road toward a common mustering point for westbound caravans. It was a perfect summer morning. The sun behind him had not crested the Mount of Olives. The cloudless sky was many shades of blue.

A crowd of people and animals marked the caravansary. Josiah picked out the girls, Kochesh, and his kinsmen. About ten others were busy checking and securing baggage on the camels.

"Where is Casil?" were Kochesh's words of greeting. Josiah hadn't seen him. "Put your things on that camel. We need to leave soon." Josiah did as directed. He looked at Jerusalem, silhouetted against the rising sun. The palace of Jehovah stood out clearly. *I will sing a song to Jehovah. I should thank Him for letting me make this journey. Who would have believed I could get a week away from home, with Hannah, with a man as great as Kochesh, in a beautiful foreign city?* He began to sing softly to himself as he looked around for Hannah.

> He brought me forth into a wide place;
> He saved me, because He delighted in me.

"At last! Get your things on that camel. Did you sleep too long? We have to get moving." Kochesh sounded irked as Casil came huffing into earshot. Everyone finished loading up and waited for Kochesh to signal them to start.

The camels carried the cargo and the people walked. Kochesh led them at a brisk pace for a while before letting them relax into a comfortable stroll. Josiah had been hurrying along beside Casil, listening to the endless woes Casil had suffered over the past three days. But finally, Josiah had a chance to join Hannah and Rachel.

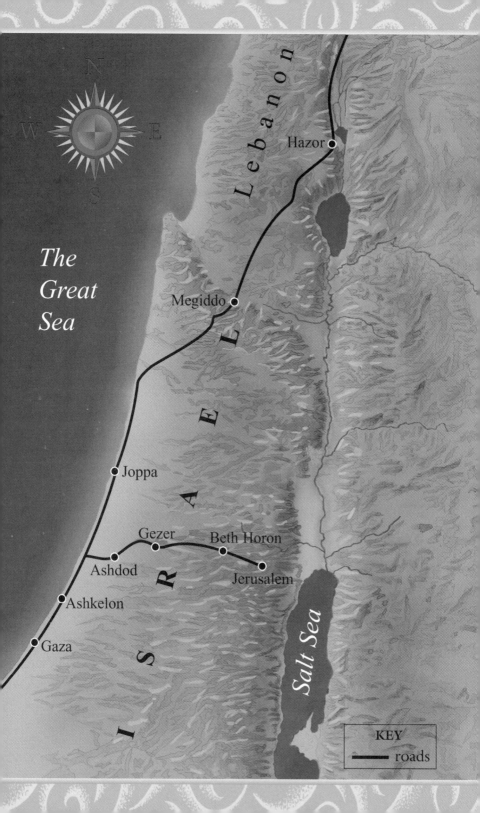

"Isn't this exciting! I still can't believe we are getting to go to the coast for an entire week. Help me get Rachel excited; she thinks it will be dull." Hannah's enthusiasm was contagious. Josiah tried to help her infect Rachel.

"If we didn't have to walk for four days, I might like it better," Rachel moaned.

"It'll do you good not to sit at home eating so much milk and honey."

"Casil!" Rachel shot after him and chased him behind a camel. Hannah and Josiah laughed after them. "They will probably have all of Joppa destroyed by the time we leave," Hannah said, giggling.

"Probably," agreed Josiah. "So much for making a good impression on the Philistines."

"Right," agreed Hannah. "What Philistines? Are these men Philistines?" She looked around at their companions.

"I meant the Philistines in Ashkelon."

"Are they in Joppa?"

"No, they're in Ashkelon. We're going to Ashkelon, not Joppa."

Hannah frowned. "My father said we were going to Joppa."

"He said the wrong place. He meant Ashkelon."

"Oh," said Hannah.

"Gezer is always full of travelers going east or west," Dagathan was saying. "We may meet up with Ammonites or Moabites, Egyptians or Phoenicians, and of course many Philistines. In Jerusalem you see the people who buy from the merchants. Out here you see the merchants in all their roughness and lowliness."

"Is there much danger from robbers?" Hannah asked.

"I haven't heard of many attacks recently. The last one I know of cost the bandits more than they gained. King Solomon keeps this road well guarded. And don't fear; our men are skilled at using force when necessary." Josiah looked around at the burly Philistines marching along, all armed with swords, spears, or bows. They did look formidable.

None of them talked much. Dagathan was apparently the only Israelite in the caravan; only he and Tashni spoke to the Levites.

"Is something wrong with Kochesh? He hasn't spoken much all day."

"His thoughts are full of the journey and matters of provision, trade, and profit. A merchant's life is often difficult. Success depends much on other people and on events in the world that no man can control."

The countryside was beautiful that time of year. Summer's lush green spread over the hills. Herds of sheep scattered over their rolling pastureland. Occasionally a small village was nestled in a fertile valley, a cluster of low white houses surrounded by grain, olive trees, and vineyards. Sharp ridges broke up the landscape and steered the travelers along the winding road toward Gezer.

Hill country gave way to the Shephelah, a band of foothills inland from Canaan's coastal plain. More sheep and cattle appeared. Crops were more frequent. Walking was easier, to Josiah's joy. They seemed to be always going down, down, downhill. Several other caravans passed them headed toward Jerusalem, and they bypassed one larger, slower group that must have left in front of them before dawn.

Kochesh stopped near the lower village of Beth Horon at midday. They rested the animals, watered them from the village well, and then spread out under a grove of trees to eat and doze through the heat. Josiah had finished eating and was enjoying having his legs still when he noticed Kochesh take Dagathan by the arm and lead him away from the others. Josiah wanted to ask Kochesh if they could all sing to pass the time.

The two men went around a small hill on the far side of the road. It was closer for Josiah to just walk over the hill, and he did. Crossing its crest, he didn't see Kochesh or Dagathan. He had gone down the slope before he heard their voices coming from behind a boulder at the base of the hill. Curiosity made him pause to listen to them before calling out; he didn't want to interrupt something private.

" . . . more than fast enough," he heard Dagathan insist. "No one will suspect trouble yet. They won't even talk before evening, if then."

"Are you sure?" Kochesh snapped.

"Yes! They are all working the day away. And there is no reason for them to become suspicious. Besides, at the rate you are pulling us, we'll reach Gezer well before the sun is gone."

"Very well, then. Everyone can finish their naps."

"Come on. You need a nap yourself. You see dangers that aren't there."

As the men's voices moved, Josiah realized that in a few steps his eavesdropping would be discovered. Thinking quickly, he decided to bluff. "Kochesh?" he called inquisitively, starting to walk down the hill and looking the other way, as if straining to see something.

"Josiah!" Kochesh shouted in surprise. Josiah turned toward him and smiled.

"There you are. I was, I was looking for you, and I couldn't find you. I didn't know you were—"

"What do you want?" Kochesh interrupted.

"Ah, I just wondered if you were here. And I wanted to ask if we could sing while we walk, when we start again."

Kochesh broke into his familiar beaming smile. "Yes, yes, we can sing. When all are rested and revived, we will resume our journey, and we will sing."

"A marvelous idea," Dagathan agreed. He suggested they all three take rest in sleep with the others.

Camels and men stirred to life a short while later. The sun had started its journey back down to the west, but it was still hot. The travelers spread their head cloths wide to deflect its rays from their skin.

Josiah had lain on a patch of grass, unable to sleep. His mind was working over what he had heard; who was working too much to talk about something they shouldn't be suspicious of anyway? Furthermore, why did getting to Gezer matter so much? Now he watched closely as the Philistines loaded baggage back onto their beasts. Did those bags contain stolen property?

Casil was full of chatter now. He seemed so excited about reaching Ashkelon! Josiah was excited too, but he got tired of hearing his friend rattle on about swords, shields, gold, jewels, and all.

When he got a chance, Josiah reminded Kochesh about singing to pass the time. The half-Philistine turned to the full Philistines and said a few sentences in their language. Josiah caught a few words and phrases, but not enough to make sense of it. Whatever Kochesh said, he drew laughter from the men. Kochesh then drew a deep breath and thundered out a song in Philistine. The others joined him, with some higher voices singing a counterpart.

It wasn't the best quality music Josiah had ever heard, but he was intrigued by its difference. The tune was simple and the words fairly repetitive. After listening through a few rounds, Josiah joined the main part. Philistine was close enough to Hebrew that he could follow the song. A few words were strange, and he didn't have the accent right, but Kochesh laughed and nodded encouragingly for him to continue.

On they sang as the land rolled to the edge of the Shephelah. The sun was in their eyes when they finally saw the hill of Gezer in the distance. Kochesh stopped them outside the city and went in alone. Many people were around the city gate. Josiah and his friends left the Philistines to tend their camels and went to look down onto the plain.

Gezer was a fortified city in a strategic location. The road that Kochesh's caravan had just taken was a main route from the coastal road into the interior cities of Israel and to Jerusalem itself. Gezer overlooked part of the widest stretch of the great coastal plain. Josiah looked down on one of the world's most crucial trade (and invasion) routes, the one large roadway from Africa through Canaan into Syria. It was the only major route joining Mesopotamia and Anatolia with Africa, the three homes of the world's mightiest nations. And Solomon's Israel sat on top of it.

"Where are we sleeping tonight?" Rachel wondered. None of them knew, but Casil answered anyway. "We'll take a space inside the city, up against the wall. Caravans always spend the night next to the wall."

Other caravans crawled along the distant road from north and south, trying to reach Gezer by nightfall. A large group had just come uphill from the plain. Josiah thought they had a wild look to them; not Egyptian, but definitely desert dwellers.

"Is that the way to Joppa?" Hannah pointed to the northbound road.

"Yes," Casil and Josiah answered together. "But we're going the other way, south to Ashkelon," Casil continued.

The sound of hooves stopped Hannah from asking another question. They turned to see Dagathan mounted high on a camel. One of the Philistine retainers rode another. Each led a second, empty camel. "Let's go, Levites. You girls join Loth and me, and you boys get on these empty camels."

"Why the hurry?" Josiah asked as he clambered up the flank of the camel tethered to Dagathan's.

"We have to make camp for the night. Kochesh wants you back." Casil was atop the camel Loth led, and Rachel rode behind Loth. Hannah perched behind Dagathan, and away they went.

Josiah tried to sit on his mount the proper way, but he had never ridden much, certainly not camels. Their humped backs and ungainly stride kept a rider from straddling a camel as he would a donkey or horse. Josiah sat with his legs together off to one side of the beast and his torso turned slightly to face forward. He held on to the rope harness with all his might.

Dagathan led them at a canter through the pockets of caravaneers scattered around the hill of Gezer. Josiah looked up at the walls of the city far above him. He couldn't imagine being an enemy soldier who had to attack those walls.

He didn't want to be a camel-rider either. He felt his bones rattle from the jarring and wobbling. He looked at Hannah in front of him, riding behind Dagathan. She saw him and waved, looking like she was having great fun. Josiah didn't want to release his grip to wave back.

After circling halfway around the hill, they came to a spot some distance from any other group. Kochesh had had his men set up camp there. The camels lay in a ring, like spokes on a wheel. Inside that ring was a ring of ten small tents. In the center were two larger tents.

"Good! Make ready for bed. We all need to get to sleep so we can start at dawn tomorrow and get to Ashkelon with daylight remaining." Kochesh seemed very alert and did not smile. He assured them they could wash in the morning; it would help them wake up, he declared. But now they had to go to bed and to sleep right away.

Dagathan would sleep in one of the big tents with Josiah and Casil, Tashni in the other with Hannah and Rachel. The men and presumably Kochesh would take the two-man tents surrounding them. Josiah noticed that the camels were already asleep. From a jar of water someone had brought from a nearby stream he washed off his head, hands, and feet before stretching out inside the goatskin tent. As he lay down, he realized how tired he was.

The camp soon fell quiet as his body slowly relaxed. It was hard to fall asleep immediately because he was so tired. He remained alert enough to hear voices outside, one of which was Kochesh's. Casil was breathing deeply, nearly snoring. Dagathan lay still and quiet. It was dark inside the enclosed tent, though Josiah didn't know if it were totally dark outside.

"I assure you we have only twenty men and such goods as I am permitted. My sister and her husband and my wife and I make this journey regularly." Kochesh's voice had risen enough that

Josiah could understand. Other voices answered too low to be intelligible. Josiah lay dozing for a moment until the words of Kochesh registered as odd. Curiosity woke him up again.

Kochesh was saying something else. Josiah sat up and softly moved toward the tent flap.

"What's wrong, Josiah?" Dagathan whispered.

"Nothing," Josiah whispered back and left the tent. He looked toward the voices and saw a half-dozen figures moving in the dark gray twilight. A hand gripped his arm.

"Do you need something?" Dagathan asked, still whispering.

"Who are they?" Josiah asked.

"Who?" He looked, still holding Josiah's arm. Kochesh and a Philistine stood together. Four men had mounted horses and were trotting away. Josiah saw the distinctive lines of helmets and sheathed swords.

"Just guards from Gezer making sure we are safe for the night. Don't worry; just lie back down and get your sleep." Dagathan gently pulled Josiah back into the tent.

Notes to the Reader

Solomon's Palace Complex

First Kings 7:1 records that King Solomon spent thirteen years building his own house. This house was probably a group of buildings analogous to the "houses" in this story, but on a much larger scale. The house of the Forest of Lebanon was a part of this larger complex along with the porch, throne room, and courtyard described in I Kings 7.

The story imagines detail that Scripture does not record. The exact function of the house of the Forest is not clear, but given its design it was most likely a place for repose and conversation rather than living or meeting on a large scale. Without doubt it was very beautiful. The description of its stonework implies that the building stones were of a special kind, perhaps marble or colored granite, cut to fit and polished. The cedar interior would have been ornate, elegant, and fragrant. A later reference mentions that the golden shields of the temple were kept here; it is not certain they were there in Solomon's time. But the house would have been near to the temple, so it is perfectly possible that storage of temple instruments was one of its functions from the beginning.

Animals in the Ancient World

First Kings 10:22 reports that the merchant navy Solomon sent to Tarshish brought back precious metals and animals. The exact meaning of these Hebrew words is uncertain, but "apes and peacocks" is plausible. Ancient civilizations were in constant contact and prized animals highly. The Egyptians were known for keeping exotic African animals. It would be no surprise if the market of an important trade center like Jerusalem had rare animals on display and even up for sale.

Review and Discussion

1. How does Adaiah, Josiah's father, feel about King Solomon's marrying foreign wives?

2. Josiah says that he can play a song without thinking about it and still make the hearers feel its full impact. Is he right?

3. What is the author's purpose for describing Josiah's view of the snake and ape?

4. What is the significance of the color red?

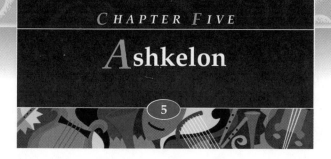

CHAPTER FIVE

Ashkelon

5

Kochesh woke them all while it was still dark. He hurried them through their preparations and led them out to the road without even allowing them to eat or bathe, as he had said he would. His explanation was that he had slept longer than intended. If that was true, Josiah was glad for the extra sleep. *I couldn't survive getting up earlier than this. Why the rush? We got to Gezer in daylight. Ashkelon is no farther away, and it's supposed to be easier traveling.* He grumpily marched along beside a camel. Josiah hadn't been awake that early for a year, so it was no wonder he was upset. In contrast, Hannah always seemed to be cheerful. The only person she could find to talk to was Tashni. The two women made the only sound besides the scuff of shoes and hooves.

Canaan's coastal plain was a black blanket stretching to the horizon. As the sun climbed behind them, the titanic shadow of the Shephelah foothills rolled back to expose a fertile green plain. Josiah's mood improved as they passed grain fields, olive groves, and flower patch after flower patch. The road was level, and the going was easy.

"Welcome to Philistia," said the voice of Dagathan beside him.

"It's beautiful," Josiah replied.

Casil made no effort to hide his delight. "Beautiful? This is magnificent! Grand! The greatness of greatnesses! No rocks or mountains or pits. Just endless, awesome green!"

He wasn't quite correct about the lack of rocks, mountains, and pits, but the plain was a far cry from the mountainous terrain around Jerusalem. A few streams watered the land, and wells were shallower and plentiful.

"Josiah," Hannah said a short while after, "are we completely outside of Israel now?"

"Yes, we are. This is Philistine country. They live from Joppa, a whole day's journey north, to Gaza, another day's journey south of Ashkelon."

"Is it true that they come from over the sea, a long way to the west?"

"So they say. Wouldn't it be fun to take a ship across the sea to some other land where nothing is the same as it is here? A land full of sea monsters and wild men and cities made of diamonds?" Josiah looked to the sky.

"I don't know what wild men would be doing with diamond cities, and sea monsters don't sound like fun to me. But it would be exciting to travel on a ship. Maybe we can come back to the sea someday." Hannah paused. "Josiah," she went on in a different tone. Josiah, wondering what she had meant by *we,* was hardly listening. "Something about this trip troubles me. Do you know what I mean? Things keep happening that seem strange. Did you notice? We never met any Israelite merchants, and now we are out of Israel and in Philistia. These men whisper to each other but don't talk aloud. I tried to ask one about his camel, just to start a conversation, but he just smiled this odd smile and wouldn't say anything."

"Maybe he was embarrassed to talk to such a beautiful woman," Josiah offered, and was instantly embarrassed himself.

"No," Hannah continued without seeming to notice, "it was more like he was getting away with something and was trying not to laugh. Like asking about a camel was the silliest thing I could do."

"Maybe he didn't know what to say."

"But it's more than that. Am I being foolish? Haven't you noticed?"

"No, no. I mean no, you aren't being foolish, but no, I haven't noticed. The Philistines are odd; that's the only problem. Dagathan and Tashni are friendly, aren't they?"

"Yes, they are. Tashni isn't the kind of woman I'm used to, but she is a Philistine."

"Half Philistine," Josiah corrected. "She's Kochesh's sister. I guess I should say that makes her 'all Philistine and all Israelite.' " Even as he laughed at his own joke, Josiah began to turn over in his mind what Hannah had said. She had noticed things he hadn't, and he had not mentioned the two snatches of conversation he'd caught. Last night came to his mind. Israelite soldiers, certainly. Twenty men. My *wife* and I, Kochesh had said, hadn't he? Or had he said my *men* and I? The words were similar. Maybe Kochesh's trace of accent had made it sound like *wife*. But what Kochesh said to Dagathan at their rest stop yesterday—that was mysterious, and there was no doubt what words he used.

He thought for a while until the unfamiliar sights and smells of Philistia drew his attention away. The people wore clothes of a different cut and pattern than was common in Jerusalem. There seemed to be a lot of patterned outfits with images of birds, fish, and other animals. The smell of trees and flowers was suddenly cut with a nasty odor. "Hey, look at those!" Casil called, pointing. Josiah saw a small herd of freshly shorn sheep.

"They've already shorn their sheep?" he asked aloud. Casil and the Philistines laughed aloud. "Those are pigs, you mountain goat!" Casil politely informed him. *They are pigs,* Josiah thought, feeling slight revulsion. The pigs' pinkish-white skin was littered with black patches. One of the men said something about being hungry. Josiah couldn't think of eating the nasty, smelly creatures. He'd have preferred tree bark.

They passed the great Philistine city of Ashdod around midday, but Kochesh didn't want to stop there. He led them on until another smell blew into their faces from straight-ahead. It was hot, past midday, and they were all tired. But the peculiar smell seemed to stir the Philistines to walk faster and talk more. Josiah knew the smell was familiar, but he couldn't place it until they walked over a low slope into full view of the sea.

A coastal road joined theirs from north and south. Kochesh called it a good time to break their trip. After settling the camels, the Philistines all went down to the narrow strip of white sand and waded into the sea.

Josiah remembered the seashore from Joppa, three years ago. His friends were as delighted as he was. Rachel had never seen the sea.

"Isn't it beyond words?" Kochesh asked Josiah. "My people use music and poetry to describe the sea; speech is insufficient. She is the kingdom no man can rule, the heart of the power of the gods, and the unbounded road to fortune and glory. A long way from the dusty heights of Jerusalem." Kochesh acted like himself for the first time in their journey.

After cooling themselves in the surf and napping, they began the final leg of their journey to Ashkelon. Kochesh had driven them longer than usual so that they could break at the seaside. Consequently they were starting later in the day, but the distance to go was comparatively short and easy.

Josiah saw the most incredible bands of merchants, soldiers, and dignitaries now. A troop of Philistine soldiers marched past. A long line of camels sauntered by under guide of men Kochesh identified as Midianites. A Tyrian emissary with a mounted retinue forty-strong passed. Out to sea, tiny fishing boats flecked the blue water. Inland it was drier, with fewer trees and fields.

The sun was descending toward the sea when Kochesh's men cheered for joy. One hefted Josiah into the air to give him his first look at Ashkelon. Josiah saw only a short gray line beside the sea.

As they moved closer, it grew into one of the most impressive sights Josiah had ever seen. All around, the land was flat. Out of the ground rose a massive wall of earth. Running from the edge of the beach, it curved out of sight far to the left. At the foot of the wall palm trees three times taller than Kochesh looked like grass beside a house. A chain of big, boxy towers loomed from atop the wall. The coastal road ran right into the foot of the wall before wrapping around the city to continue its voyage south on the far side. A path sloped at an angle up to the north gate, set between two of the towers.

"Behold Ashkelon, the great city! Come, friends, let me lead you into the garden of Philistia." The Philistines were already moving ahead. Josiah watched the men rush to a low, wide structure at the foot of the path. Kochesh headed to the same place. When Josiah asked why they had to stop there, Kochesh explained that they had to give thanks for a safe journey and return to Ashkelon.

"Give thanks to whom?" Josiah wanted to know.

"To the god," he was told.

A crowd milled about the building's entrance. That odd, stimulating kind of music, the kind that Kochesh had played with Josiah's harp at the festival, wafted out of its windows and over the people. Josiah and Casil followed Kochesh inside. Sharp incense filled the air. They stood in a spacious room before a huge curtain embroidered with trees, animals, and human figures. A stone altar jutted through the center of the curtain. Men were paying money to several attendants, maybe priests, Josiah thought. After paying, they would go to the altar and raise their arms, then bow down in a peculiar fashion. Josiah watched several of Kochesh's men, then Kochesh himself, complete the ceremony. Josiah peered at the altar to make out what was on it: the shiny silver head and shoulders of a tiny metal bull poked out of a stone enclosure on top of the altar.

Outside, Josiah asked what that had all been about. "That is a shrine to the god Bull," Kochesh told him. "We give an offering to him for protecting us along the way. It's a Philistine custom going back many centuries. Wouldn't an Israelite give thanks to Jehovah for a safe journey?"

"Yes, I suppose," Josiah answered.

They got the caravan going and continued up the zigzagging ascent. Hannah asked Josiah what was in the low building; she had overheard what it was, but hadn't looked inside. "It's just a little house for a Philistine god. They go in, give some money, make a bow, and go out."

"What is in there? What do they bow to?"

The Northern Gate
of Ashkelon

"A little silver bull."

"A bull? Josiah, that's an idol! It's another god!"

"They're Philistines. This is Philistia. Philistines serve their own god."

"I know. I guess I just never really expected to see it."

"The king's wives serve other gods. They have altars for them right around Jerusalem, so it's not as though it's all that strange or foreign."

"You're right," she conceded. "I just realize how different it will be on the other side of that wall."

"It is not that different," he returned, annoyed with her. "They have their own god. They have their own city. They have their own ways."

He waited to enter the gate, straining to look up at the two guard towers, when Hannah said, "Turn around." He did, and nearly lost his balance. You could see *forever* from up there! The plain spread out below him in a panorama of greens and browns. To his right, the Shephelah blanketed the land, and on the horizon he could see the hills of Judea. "How far can you see from here?" he murmured.

"From the top of the watch towers, on a clear day you can see past Joppa, a long day's journey north," called Dagathan. "If not for the hills, you could see Gezer."

"No one slips up on this city," Casil observed.

They turned their backs on the view and entered Ashkelon.

Eight persons reclined around a delicious meal in the court-yard of an opulent house that evening. Kochesh, Dagathan, Tashni, and their four Levite charges were the guests of Abdod, a Philistine of some rank and means. After depositing his camels and merchandise in a merchants' corral, Kochesh had led his young guests through the vibrant, noisy marketplace, and all along he greeted a seemingly endless stream of friends. He finally finished and brought them to this fine three-story house in Ashkelon's richest quarter.

"Are not the sons of Levi dedicated to the ministration of your God?" rumbled the lordly Abdod.

"Yes," Casil answered. "Levites take care of the palace of Jehovah and all the houses around it. We manage all the offerings and the tithes that come in. We even keep everything secure and orderly. And most importantly, we provide all the music." Casil beamed.

"The ministration of Jehovah depends on the Levites, my lord," Kochesh supported.

Abdod looked impressed. "Excellent! Ashkelon is immensely honored by your presence. Our people are zealous devotees of every vintage of the finest poetry, music, and art. The exaltation of deity is a superlative venue for the expression of the utmost passions of the soul. And what utterance surpasses the poetic word, fitly framed, swathed in the jeweled shimmering robes of stately music?"

"Right!" agreed Casil.

"Now enlighten me, please," Abdod continued, "as to what in-terests incited youths to so great a traversal? Holiday? Adventure? Exile? Connivance of one *Kochesh?*"

Casil failed to answer this time, so Josiah spoke up instead. "We want to see the musicians of your city and hear them play. Kochesh tells us the greatest musicians from all nations can be found here."

"Connivance of a Kochesh, then. Very well! Our premiere minstrels you shall know. The morrow offers a timely treat. The Sacred Ones will sing together throughout the morning in antici-pation of evening festivities. I see that the god has brought you to our house at a most appropriate moment to fulfill your desires."

Conversation changed to Jerusalem, what they had seen on their journey, and what business Kochesh had before him—Josiah remembered afterward only that he sought certain high-priced musical instruments for his return. Not long after finishing his meal, Josiah's eyes began to shut. Though Abdod seemed willing to talk indefinitely, Kochesh finally thanked him and asked that they be shown to bed.

Josiah awoke to see blue sky glowing outside the windows. His bedroom was on the top floor, wonderfully quiet and cooled by steady sea breezes. Surprisingly, Casil was already gone. A water basin and a handful of sea salt had been brought for Josiah to wash with, and a tunic and robe from his pack were laid out. They had been perfumed, he noticed. Manly spices, fortunately; nothing effeminate. Clearly, some servant had been up working early to get his things ready. That all this had been brought in without waking him testified to just how tired he had been.

When he had finished washing and dressing, Josiah walked out onto the mezzanine and looked down into the gardens of the courtyard. Abdod's house was nearly as big as the Garnet! He found a stairway up to the roof. Unlike Jerusalem, Ashkelon was flat. Josiah looked around at the giant cup full of white roofs within a chalky-white brim. The earthen wall, topped by a stone wall, looked even more impressive now that he could see how much area it surrounded. The wall ran straight along the shore. From the northern entrance they had used yesterday, the wall swung inland in a great half-circle far to the south to rejoin the sea wall at the southern gate. Abdod's house was near the sea wall and not far from some large buildings Josiah supposed to be the royal palace and the palace of their god, either Dagon or the "Bull god."

Hunger reminded him there was more to life than sightseeing. He went downstairs in search of food and was not disappointed. Kochesh and Casil were finishing breakfast when he joined them. "Dagathan is completing some business for me so that I can take you to hear the Sacred Ones sing. I should be able to take you through the palace and into the chambers of the masters. Didn't you eat enough last night? A man would think we starved you all the way from Jerusalem!" Josiah had torn into breakfast like a lion.

Casil was impatient to go. He hurried Josiah through his meal and was out the door before Kochesh and Josiah had their shoes strapped on. "I hope that scamp falls down a well," Kochesh muttered, then looked at Josiah and smiled.

Kochesh led them to the palace complex of the king of Ashkelon. He explained that the girls had left earlier with Tashni on some "women's business" and would meet them in the house of Song. They passed guards in glimmering iron armor into halls and courtyards with massive pillars and carved stone statues. The contrast with Jehovah's palace was striking: Josiah couldn't help staring at the sculptures and wall friezes of men and women engaged in what looked like huge dances. The painting vibrated with a feel of vividness and reality that Josiah found fascinating.

Music burst from a door ahead. A choir had started a song with a scintillatingly fast pace. Kochesh directed them to lean into the doorway. They saw an enclosed room full of a hundred or more men singing. "The Sacred Ones," Kochesh whispered in Josiah's ear. The men wore red loincloths and golden belts. They sang with great energy, following a choirmaster who kept the beat and occasionally cued parts. Their piece developed into an intricate arrangement of competing parts—basically like what palace Levites sang, but with a driving rhythm that rose to an exhilarating climax and then gently fell into a tender lullaby.

"Oooh-waah!" Casil sighed. "That was the highest! How many men do you have like them?"

"Several hundred. And many women who are also quite good, for women. Come; let's go to meet one of the masters."

A fountain of water cascaded down a staircase into a pool of clean water. The pool was ringed with olive trees and milk-white stones. Casil pointed out another of those fancy poles like the ones at the youth festival and in the court of the Garnet. "What are those?" Josiah asked him.

"Symbols of the renewal of life," Casil answered grandly. "They're indispensable to Philistine worship."

How would you know? thought Josiah. "Casil, why do you think they are showing us such honor?"

"They appreciate us! They know we have talent in music and want to make friends with us. Unlike our *master* Johanon, they know music of all kinds."

"We're just children, really. To them, anyway, we're just children."

"Speak for yourself. We are the most skilled music students among all the Levites. The palace singers are too fat from the tithes and offerings to—" Casil broke off as Kochesh approached.

"The master wants to see you. Come, and act as impressively as possible."

The master was a sharp-eyed man with no hair. He appraised the two Israelites and let them be seated. "So your name is Casil? Are you a skilled minstrel, Casil?" Casil assured him that he was and started to elaborate, but the master looked at Josiah. "And you are Josiah. Are you skilled with music, Josiah?"

"Jehovah has given me a gift for music," Josiah responded reflexively.

"Jehovah? So you believe music gifts come from the gods. Do you suppose you could receive a gift from another god, as well?"

Josiah laughed uncertainly. "I suppose I would take any gift given to me."

"Very good! When can I hear your skill?" the master asked, looking at both boys.

"At the evening festivities perhaps Josiah and Casil and the young women who came with them could treat us to some music," Kochesh said.

"Splendid!" agreed the master.

When they went back to the practice rooms in the house of Song, they found Hannah and Rachel waiting. The girls were listening to a chorus of women sing a voice exercise that sounded like an unending wail. It was intricate and showed the women's skill but was not very pleasant.

"Josiah!" Hannah called out upon seeing him. She asked Kochesh if they could please go outside. Kochesh looked bemused, but agreed. Hannah took Josiah by the arm as they went and pulled him forward. They stepped into the sunshine of a wide court full of people. Josiah noticed some curious glances, and wondered what was so important that Hannah had to act like this.

"Josiah, I don't want to be in this palace anymore. Did you see how lewd some of these statues are? Or what's on the wall paintings? Or that in every room there is an idol altar?"

"What? No, I haven't. You're acting silly. I'm sure they have idols of their gods, but you knew that. But just because we're not used to their art does not mean it's so bad. What lewd statues?"

Rachel had slipped up to them. "They're really strange," she said. "There are all these statues of women and men with no clothes on!"

"Don't you two know who made the first statue without clothes on? Jehovah did! He made Man out of clay, and He didn't make him with a nice, long white robe on! So what's so evil about statues?"

"But, Josiah, it's just that—" Hannah started.

"That you've never seen it before," Josiah finished for her. "Listen, we are here to learn about music, and while you were both off wandering, Casil and I met one of their master musicians. Leave statues to the sculptors; let's hear music!"

He left them to rejoin Kochesh and Casil.

Kochesh decided it was time to see more of Ashkelon, so out of the palace they went and into the heart of the city. The five of them walked along the spectacular canals, pools, and fountains Ashkelon was famous for. A river of water came right out of the ground through the city's huge wells, flooding its extensive waterworks. The water was cold and clear. It felt great outside and inside the body, since the day was getting hot.

They went to the Sea Gate and walked out to the edge of the great ramp that slid down to Ashkelon's docks. Kochesh pointed out the various ships and where they were from. "That one is

Grecian. Those three are from Egypt, probably loaded with grain. That one, and that one, are from Cyprus. That big one must be full of metal to be riding so low in the water."

"Have you ever been over the sea?" Casil asked Kochesh.

"Oh, yes. I have been to Greece several times. Grecians believe that each city should rule itself, like in Philistia, so there is no one king. Each city is different, having its own treasures and pleasures."

"I would like to go to Greece, or Egypt, or even Tarshish!" Casil looked eagerly toward the horizon.

"Why?" Rachel wanted to know.

"Because they're different! Because they see things differently. They know things we don't know and can do things we can't do."

"There is a lot to learn from the experience and labor of other nations," Josiah agreed. "Just by observing, we can gain knowledge that they paid the real price for."

"Well said, Josiah!" Kochesh praised. "And you can do just that this evening at the festivities. Now let me teach you something about Philistine food."

"What are the 'festivities' we're going to tonight?" Hannah asked.

Kochesh walked toward the gate. "A happy occasion, such as Ashkelon has many of. You will enjoy it, I vow!"

They ate in the market and returned to the house of Abdod to rest. Later, back at the palace of Dagon (as they had learned it was), they listened to the huge choirs preparing for the evening. A large orchestra was also assembled and readying itself. Josiah looked upward at the lofty ceiling supported by huge columns and thought of Samson. He imagined the beams and panels falling down onto the crowd. He didn't think this palace looked like it could collapse that way, but he was glad they no longer fought Philistines, just the same.

At Kochesh's suggestion Josiah had brought his harp from Abdod's house. In fact, they all had brought their instruments, and took to cleaning and tuning them. The harp had not been struck for several days. It had spent the entire journey from Jerusalem wrapped tightly in a sack on a camel. Josiah now lovingly checked over every bit of it and carefully adjusted the strings until it sang true.

Hordes of people filled the palace grounds for the festivities. A huge decorated pole was set atop the main altar, a polished stone edifice crowned with silver. Companies of servants brought food and drink while the priests and their attendants (Josiah thought of his father) readied some animals for sacrifice. Then came the Sacred Ones, beginning to fill the air with cheerful, absorbing music.

The sun was just above the sea wall when the festivities began. Song, theatrics, and unfamiliar rituals swirled together in an amazing display. Josiah was truly impressed. For an event they supposedly did often, it was complicated. Of course, as he realized, it could all be in a completely different order without seeming any different to him. He couldn't follow a progression from one part to the next until they reached something similar to the enactment he had seen at the youth festival outside of Jerusalem; a kingly character everyone adored took on a black-clad villain and was overpowered. As they withdrew from sight, Kochesh appeared and told the Levites to follow him.

He led them to a spot near other instrument players and took up a large stringed instrument himself. Motioning the four Israelites to do likewise, he joined in the sad, mournful lamentation that was filling the scene in the aftermath of the defeat of Dagon by Death. The music built to a climax and fell off.

Suddenly Kochesh signaled Josiah. "Fill the silence!" he ordered. "Make them all cry!" Josiah balked, but Kochesh gestured at Josiah's harp insistently. The orchestra was very subdued, and the choirs quiet.

Josiah closed his eyes and thought of sadness, then planned his first chords. He began a dirge so melancholy he was soon wet-eyed. So absorbed was Josiah in his task, he didn't realize that over two thousand Philistines were listening intently.

He finished, and after a long silence a single reed pipe announced the beginning of the resolution. The goddess character, Asherah, eventually appeared and went about her rescue mission. She finally returned joyfully with the liberated Dagon, having defeated Death again. As the two characters embraced, Kochesh signaled Josiah to begin another solo. Josiah played a spirited melody. It was shorter this time; the orchestra broke out in full force with lots of booming and crashing. The worshipers became noisy, then outright rowdy. Josiah saw Dagon and Asherah begin a dance together, and wondered how much remained until the end. But Kochesh gripped his shoulders and turned him around, beaming. "Splendid artistry! That was your very heart coming out. Well done, all of you. What little remains concerns a final sacrifice to Dagon, the sort of affair Israelites have no interest in. Come on, all, let's return to the house of Lord Abdod." He was already herding them toward the nearest gate. "We'll have another hearty meal, and a good sleep, and another great day in Ashkelon!"

The next morning, Josiah walked among the bazaars in the market of Ashkelon remembering the previous night's sights and sounds. Philistine music was different: it was powerful, it was freer than the music at the palace of Jehovah. He grinned as he thought of evoking sadness in a crowd of Israelites like he had in the Philistines. Then again, there was the Day of Atonement, when music matched the Scripture's instructions to weep in sorrow for sin. Maybe, thought Josiah, on the next Day of Atonement he could make Israelites cry! He laughed as he thought of Johanon's reaction. He could hear his teacher saying . . . *but never mind Johanon; old men never changed.*

He was accompanying Kochesh on a search for special instruments to take back to sell in Jerusalem. He was also getting a lesson on musical instruments as they surveyed devices of every shape and size from twenty different lands. Josiah was soon absorbed in an artist's bliss of handling and testing instruments.

Kochesh had a deep knowledge of musical hardware and a determination to wrestle bargains away from his fellow merchants. Josiah thought he seemed absolutely ruthless when it came to dragging shekels off the price of his purchases.

After a while, Josiah was encumbered with two hefty stringed instruments, lyres. He followed Kochesh to the last of the shops. It was then he saw the last man on earth he expected to see: down one street, a block away, tall and lean with a gray-streaked beard, and even wearing the loose robes of an Israelite—Nahath, Hannah's father. Josiah was enough astounded at the likeness to stare, but the man vanished into the crowd. Josiah laughed at himself as he followed Kochesh into the shop. Israelites were readily at hand in the city; he had seen several that morning, all merchants seeking the same sort of profit as Kochesh. And all bearded, and all in the same style of robe.

Josiah had never seen Kochesh happier than he was when they returned their morning's plunder to storage at Abdod's and went inside to repose. "What prizes!" Kochesh cooed. "What prizes! I'll earn a thousand gold shekels and more! All by the end of the month."

"What are we doing the rest of the day?" Josiah asked.

"Lord Abdod has invited you to play for him in the open court of the house of Song this afternoon. You can do whatever you like before and after. Tonight, we have a banquet here."

"What *is* Abdod?"

"He is a ruler of this city, one of the counselors to the king. He does you great honor by asking to hear you play."

Josiah took a bite from a fig and chewed a few times. "Kochesh, why is a ruler of the Philistines doing me such an honor? What does he want us to do? Are we supposed to be so impressed with Philistia we don't think of you as enemies anymore?"

"Exactly. You and I can bridge our two peoples and give them understanding of each other. We can encourage peace, love, trade . . . " Kochesh stroked one of his new lyres and smiled a businessman's smile.

At that moment Casil entered. He looked mischievously at Josiah, but before he said anything Kochesh asked him, "So, have you seen the instrument makers' house? What did you think of it, and where is Dagathan now?"

"Who knows where Dagathan is? He left me before we got back here. But the instrument makers' house is great. It's the kind of place I might like to stay for a while."

Had Josiah not been preoccupied, he might have noticed the peculiarity in Casil's manner.

The girls and Tashni returned not long after Casil, having completed a mission to the house of a well-known woman who trained the female singers and actors for the palace of Dagon. Rachel had plenty to say about the shocking appearance and behavior of the young women students. She acknowledged, however, that they had impressive vocal skills. Hannah said little, only agreeing that the young singers were well trained.

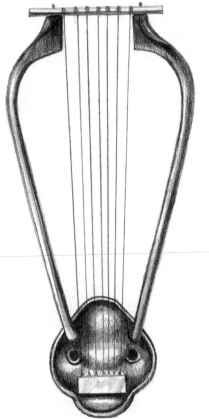

Kochesh took them all back to the house of Song that afternoon but entered through a small side gate and bypassed the areas they had seen the day before. He led them into a small private court in the northern quarter of the palace. There they waited until joined by a group of palace musicians. These musicians said they were to play with the Levites out in the public portico and wanted to practice with them first.

It was apparent that they were not accustomed to playing the kind of music Josiah and his friends were familiar with, but they seemed to have fun trying.

Finally, someone announced that Lord Abdod had arrived and was waiting in the portico.

They walked down a long hallway and up a flight of stairs onto the balcony above a three-sided courtyard whose missing wall opened to the street. Quite a large group of servants, musicians, and other palace persons were on the second-story mezzanine around them, but Josiah's eyes were drawn across the lake of people covering the courtyard below. It was a huge, bustling crowd of expectant people.

The Israelites listened as the Philistines began alone, playing a happy summer melody to get everyone in good spirits. Their leader had agreed that the Levites would start with a popular tune, which the Philistines would pick up and follow. Josiah led a song his mother had taught him years ago, one every Israelite knew and which the Philistines seemed to recognize.

Next, the Philistine group played a song that was sprightly, energetic, moving the crowd to sway with the music and clap their hands. Josiah countered with a merry tune, which the Philistines joined and accelerated. Josiah, not to be outdone, accelerated the tune even faster, then faster until it was not so much enjoyable as impressive. He outpaced the others without missing a note, drawing a round of hoots as he finished with flourish.

Now the Philistines began a song. They led the people in singing a polyphony, having the crowd respond with simple choruses as the musicians sang the verses of a poem about Dagon and the Bull god. It had something to do with a hunt: it was exciting, sometimes funny, and built to a rousing climax. Josiah surprised everyone by cutting in with a rapid countermelody so intricately woven into the music he amazed even himself that he had done it without prior practice.

Josiah determined to show them once and for all: he summoned to mind his own composition with all its passion, tension, and triumph. He plunged into it masterfully. The other Levites helped some, but it was new to them. The Philistines didn't join, for once; they only listened as Josiah began to sing.

I will love thee, O LORD, my strength.

I will call upon the LORD, who is worthy to be praised: so shall I be saved from mine enemies.

The sorrows of death compassed me, and the floods of ungodly men made me afraid.

Then the earth shook and trembled; the foundations also of the hills moved and were shaken, because he was wroth.

There went up smoke out of his nostrils, and fire out of his mouth devoured: coals were kindled by it.

Yea, he sent out his arrows, and scattered them; and he shot out lightnings, and discomfited them.

Then the channels of waters were seen, and the foundations of the world were discovered at thy rebuke, O LORD, at the blast of the breath of thy nostrils.

He sent from above, he took me, he drew me out of many waters.

Finishing, letting his hearers down from the heights, Josiah exhaled slowly with deep satisfaction. After awed silence, the crowd burst into exultation. Their musicians joined in praise that went on and on. Josiah flushed. He had *never* known such an outpouring of appreciation.

Abdod invited them back to another private court within the palace. The women disappeared when Josiah wasn't looking, but Casil and Kochesh were still there. A servant poured Josiah a drink of a reddish liquid with sweet taste that warmed his insides all the way down to his stomach. Kochesh and Abdod were animated, obviously happy, and kept saying how amazed they were at the Levites' talents. "My young man, this day's happenings impress upon me how felicitous it would be for our clan to obtain and retain such precocity! Why, you could elevate the muse of thousands out of this underworld and up to the heavens. You have in your hand power to mold kingdoms of men!" Josiah laughed at the man's exaggeration, but he was flattered.

"I believe Lord Abdod is inviting you to more than a two-day visit, Josiah. What do you say? Would Ashkelon make a home for a man like you? A place that gives you your due honor and can teach you to fully utilize your gift?"

"Ashkelon is wonderful! I have enjoyed being here, and I would like to come back someday."

Casil laughed. "What are you going to do in the meantime? Go back to sitting and listening to Johanon prattle on and on?"

"Aren't you?" Josiah grinned back at his friend.

"No," Casil said.

"Josiah, you misunderstand me," Kochesh began. "I am not just offering a return visit. I am offering a life to you. Your gifts are extraordinary; with us you can become the greatest musician in all Canaan. You can sway the minds of nations with music."

"Music is the thrown spear of rhetoric," Abdod declared.

"And unlike the Levites, we know how to teach you to use it," Kochesh continued. "Ashkelon loves you. It can provide everything a man can want. Has Jerusalem set you in a prince's house? Ashkelon can. Has Jerusalem let you lead the worship of its God? Ashkelon did."

"Jerusalem never gave us anything but a hard time," Casil agreed.

Josiah returned, "Have you already made up your mind to stay? That easily?"

"Why not? Kochesh is making me a singer in the house of Song. I'll have a regular salary, a house of my own, and nothing to do but sing and play music every day. And the kind of music that is *fun!*"

"Listen please, Josiah. Your friend wants to help us bring Israel and Philistia together. I am not suggesting you break with your own people. We want you to help us reach them." Kochesh spoke earnestly.

"Why? How?"

"Because many in Israel are bigoted against all who are not of Israel. But many are not; many Israelites want what we want. But one of the most important elements in Jerusalem that resists every attempt to bring our peoples together is the Levites!" Kochesh reddened, and his voice tightened.

Abdod, unperturbed, spoke again. "You will be the rising sun of a glorious new day."

Josiah's head swam. He asked to leave, receiving permission to go after another admonition to think it through. He rose and walked outside. Naturally, Casil followed. "Don't you see what a chance we have?" he said intently. "We can live here in luxury! We can learn all kinds of music and play for the people and buy anything we want!"

"Don't you care about your father and mother?" Josiah asked.

"Yes! They will be glad for me. But even if they're not, I have to walk my own path now. We have to be men, Josiah; we can't always let other people decide what we do."

"I know. I know you're right."

Josiah spent much of that late afternoon walking alone in the marketplace of Ashkelon. As he thought, he took in the sights and sounds. Gradually, he concluded that his friends were right; this was an opportunity to do great good for many people, an opportunity the likes of which he would not have in Jerusalem.

Back at Abdod's house, he found none of the men home and didn't bother looking for the women. He climbed to the roof and looked out over the city. It was truly beautiful. The shadow of the sea wall crept toward the house. He was thinking of the sea when he realized someone was with him. Turning, he faced Hannah, who had walked up so softly he hadn't heard her. She was grave and silent, standing very close to him. He only stared at her.

"Josiah," she finally said, "why did you play your composition that way today? You wrote that to sing in the palace of Jehovah. You sang those words just to impress the people. You sang it all wrong, just to make them listen and cry and then tell you how great you are."

"Aren't you the one who wants to sing Jehovah's songs everywhere?" Josiah shot back angrily. "How is that different than singing it here, in a city, for people who enjoy it? Why can't Jehovah's song be sung for Philistines?"

Her eyes were steady. "That was not Jehovah's song," she said quietly.

Josiah turned and walked away. A wash of emotion tightened his throat as he lashed out inside against what she had said. Swallowing, he muttered, "You can leave tomorrow and go back to Jehovah's palace . . ."

"They haven't told you? I want to leave this place, but Tashni just told me Kochesh has decided to postpone leaving for two more days. She said something about his business, but I think that you . . ." She stifled the next word.

"You're staying here?"

"Only because I have to!" She shouted, something rare for Hannah.

"If you want to leave so badly, I'll show you how. If you don't want to stay with me—come on. Get Rachel and come on."

As they went downstairs, Hannah asked frustratedly, "Has nothing made you suspicious that Kochesh is not what he seems to be?" Despite his anger, Josiah's mind began to work, recalling incidents, drawing comparisons, *thinking*. What Kochesh said to the guards at Gezer. What he said to Dagathan behind the hill. How he talked about money. His reaction when he mentioned the Levites in Jerusalem.

Josiah told Hannah and Rachel that he would return soon with a way for them to leave Ashkelon. They wanted to know where he was going, but he only turned and departed. He headed out of the house and down the crowded streets toward the marketplace. He was acting more decisively and determinedly than usual.

Josiah's destination was the Foreigners' Bazaar. Israelite merchants there maintained a big house to conduct business between Philistia and their homeland. Josiah intended to find out if any caravan was leaving for Israel the next day—it was highly likely, since it was only two days until the Sabbath, when no Israelite traveled—and to arrange for the girls to go along. He assumed any merchant would agree to accept payment upon getting them to Jerusalem. *If Hannah is so narrow she won't even let me enjoy being here, I'll happily send her home.* Josiah saw the door to the house of Israel and walked purposefully toward it. He never made it inside.

A man standing near the door said his name. Josiah froze and looked at him in surprise. What he saw made no sense for a moment. But when the man stepped toward him and smiled a familiar smile, Josiah realized that it was indeed his father. The man embraced his dumbfounded son and released a relieved laugh. "How I prayed to find one of you before this day ended! We have gone through this foul city ten times. Are you well? Where are the others? Are they all right? Has anything happened? What, has someone cut out your tongue? Answer me."

"Why are you here? Is something wrong?" Josiah asked in amazement.

"I had good reason to think something is wrong; that's why I'm here. Now about Casil and those two girls? Everything is fine?"

"Yes. Yes, fine. Why did you think something is wrong? How long have you been here?"

"Come sit with me and I'll tell you. But first, why were you striding toward that den of money-lovers looking so angry?"

Josiah walked with Adaiah toward a nearby stone ledge, but said nothing. *What did this mean?* He wondered how could he possibly tell his father everything that had happened in the last four days?

They sat, and still he was silent. Adaiah waited with infuriating patience. Finally, Josiah spoke. "Kochesh isn't able to leave tomorrow like he planned. I came to see if a caravan was leaving tomorrow morning for Jerusalem."

"You were going to come home with a different caravan?"

"Right," Josiah said, looking down.

"Do the other children intend to come with you the same way? Has there been no other trouble since you came? Has this Kochesh been a good host?"

"He has been a very good host." Josiah's heart began to race. He struggled to concentrate on what he should tell his father, but his emotions were rising.

"That is truly good to hear. Hannah's father, Casil's father, and I found that his claims were not the same to us all. We were frightened that he was up to some mischief, but I suppose we must somehow have mistaken him. Perhaps it was concern over our children." He put his arm around Josiah's shoulders.

"You came all this way because of that?"

"Oh yes. Nahath and Hushai came with me, along with Shammoth and some of his guards. We were a day's journey behind, and no one along the way remembered seeing any of you. I feared you had gone to a different city, but we came here last evening and spent all of today searching."

"I saw Nahath!" Josiah blurted. "But I didn't know it was Nahath. I thought it couldn't be."

"A pity he didn't see you. It would have saved us worry."

Was it a pity he didn't see me? Josiah wondered to himself. *Maybe it was.* "No matter now," Adaiah continued. "We are staying at an inn nearby. We can all go home tomorrow morning. Let's find Nahath and Hushai and tell them."

Josiah realized his father was getting up to go with no further questions. Hushai was Rachel's father, not Casil's. Josiah wondered why Casil's father had not come with the others . . . *Casil! What do I do about Casil?*

And then Josiah wondered if he himself really wanted to leave Ashkelon.

"Casil won't go," he said.

"How's that?"

"Casil wants to stay here. They offered to make him a palace singer, and pay him, and give him his own house. He says it's time to grow up and make his own decisions." Josiah sat still, and his father looked down at him.

"And did they offer to make you a palace singer? Do they want you to stay here and use your music for the worship of Dagon or some other Baal, and of Asherah, and of the Bull?"

Josiah didn't look up. His throat tightened, so he swallowed. But before he could speak, Adaiah continued gently, "Or do they merely want you to keep singing Jehovah's psalms for the amusement of their masses?" Josiah's stomach clenched. Now he did look up, but the setting sun was behind his father's back, leaving his face shadowed.

"You were in the plaza today?"

"We were. Though far back among the throng, we had a fine view of you all. You showed great skill, the skill I am very proud resides in my son. And perhaps I know little of the ways and wisdom of music. But I know the word of Jehovah. I know it condemns the worship of all other gods because idols are lies that lead to the destruction of whoever trusts them. And I know that Jehovah is a loving God who doesn't want us fooled into elevating an idol to His side."

Adaiah's voice was gentle but firm. He read the struggle in his son's face and paused a moment before asking, "Josiah, did you turn the hearts of these people to Jehovah today, or did you build up their trust in idolatry?"

Again Josiah looked down, nearly crying, and whispered, "I'm sorry. I'm so sorry."

He rubbed the tears from his eyes as his father again settled beside him, placing his thick arm gently around his son's shoulders. "The God who forgave David can surely forgive one who profaned David's psalms, if forgiveness is what you seek. Would you do again what you did today in front of these Philistines? Do you desire to accept their offer and stay in this city?"

No, he thought at once. Taking a deep breath, he said it aloud. "In a way I want to live like these people, but . . . but I know it is wrong."

"Why?" asked Adaiah.

"Because their lifestyle is all aimed at worshiping another god. Because they want only to gain money and power. Because," and here he faced Adaiah, "because they hate the Levites!"

"They hate Jehovah whom the Levites serve. This Kochesh is a great liar, Josiah. He deceived Nahath completely, and many others besides. My son, please forgive me; I knew something was suspicious about all this, but I did not take time or trouble to protect you as I should have."

Josiah actually laughed. "I was determined to come here, Dad."

There would be opportunity to discuss that issue later, but as they both knew, more important matters were at hand. They hurried from the market toward the inn at which Adaiah, Nahath, and their party were lodged. Along the way Josiah told his father about the incidents on their journey from Jerusalem and what they had seen in Dagon's palace the night before. Adaiah guessed that at Gezer Kochesh had been intent on keeping the Levites unseen and that his argument with Dagathan had concerned the Levite parents, to whom Kochesh had elaborately lied. The Philistine had been wise to worry; that very evening Adaiah and Nahath had talked at length with Shammoth after the guard inquired why they had sent their children off with a man whom Israelite authorities suspected of smuggling. Realizing the conflicts in the stories he had told, the three men along with Hushai and four guards assembled a caravan and left the next morning.

"The problem now is getting Hannah and Rachel, and hopefully Casil, out of this city without any trouble from the Philistines," Adaiah was saying as they reached the inn. One guard of Shammoth's was there in case they had needed to leave messages for each other. Adaiah sent him to find the rest of the men and bring them back.

"If you saw us this afternoon, why were you still searching for us?" Josiah asked his father.

"We didn't know where you were staying. Every Philistine around knows about you, but we haven't found one that knew where you were lodged. So tell me, where is it?"

"At the house of Abdod, a block from the palace."

"Where are your three friends?"

"The girls are at Abdod's house. I don't know where Casil is."

They waited until Nahath, Hushai, Shammoth, and the other three Israelite soldiers returned. Josiah felt sorely conspicuous to know that they had all seen him singing for the Philistines, but no one mentioned it. It was decided they should go at once to the house of Abdod and secure the girls, hopefully also finding out where Casil was. The danger was not knowing how the Philistines would react. Though it worried him, Adaiah agreed that Josiah should enter the house alone and try to get his friends outside without alarming any Philistines.

It was dusk by the time Josiah entered Abdod's house for the last time that week. Kochesh was waiting for him. "Where were you?" he demanded.

A lie came to Josiah's lips, but looking at Kochesh made him decide on a different course. "Sorry. Are you really not returning to Jerusalem tomorrow?"

"Do you *want* me to return? Do *you* want to return?" He smiled that big smile, with a sly look in his eye.

Another lie came to mind, but again Josiah rejected it. "Yes, I do. I am not the one to stay here and play for you."

The smile faded. "Very well. We'll be able to leave the first day of next week. But Josiah," Kochesh stepped close and put his arm around him, "consider what you may lose. This chance may not return to you. The Levite masters are suspicious and envious. They want you in Jerusalem where they can control you. They may not let you come again to the freedom of Ashkelon."

Josiah thought quickly. "Are Hannah and Rachel here? I know they want to go."

"Is that it? Why, Josiah, I believe Hannah can be persuaded to remain here, if that is what you desire. I told you; I can get you anything you want."

"Perhaps I should talk to her about it."

"Do so. She is female, and females are slow to understand what is best."

"Maybe I can tell her some things she hasn't thought of."

"Good." Kochesh smiled again.

Josiah found the two girls sitting on a corner of the roof. Making sure none of the servants was nearby, he sat down with them and briefly explained what had happened. It was a lot to take in at once, of course, but they understood the most relevant part: their fathers were waiting outside the house and they had to reach them without drawing too much attention.

"Is Casil here?" Josiah asked.

"I know he came back, but I don't know where he is."

"How do we get our instruments out?" Rachel wondered. That was a good question. The rest of their things could be left behind and replaced easily enough, but the instruments were of too high a value to abandon easily.

"We'll tell Kochesh we want to play some songs while watching the sunset from on top of the sea wall," Josiah said at length. It was a weak excuse—really a poor lie—but he could think of nothing else. Hoping that they could get away without anyone seeing them, Josiah led the girls to get their instruments. Noticing the fine sword Kochesh sold him, he strapped it to his side. He then found his beautiful harp and held it against his body. *I'll never use you again like I did today,* he decided.

Kochesh was lurking around to find out what happened after the conversation with Hannah. Josiah thought of looking for a back door, but Kochesh had already seen them. "Feel an urge to practice? All three of you?" Kochesh asked, genuinely puzzled.

"No," Josiah replied, then had nothing else to say.

Kochesh searched his face, then asked, "So what were you doing?"

"Kochesh, Hannah doesn't want to stay here. She and Rachel both want to return to Israel," Josiah said suddenly.

"As long as it won't cause you too much grief, I don't care what they do. More beautiful women are easy to find in Ashkelon. I can find you two or three at any time!" Josiah was too startled by this response to react until Kochesh asked again why they had their instruments.

The interruption of a shout from one of the household servants saved Josiah from having to answer. The servant came from the foyer shouting for help and warning about an intruder. They all looked to see Nahath in the doorway. When he saw Kochesh, he scowled. "These children are leaving with us!"

"Who is restraining them?" Kochesh asked impudently.

"What's all the uproar about?" thundered Abdod, entering the room with two burly, armed servants.

"Israelite thieves, my lord!" Kochesh cried. "This one forced his way into the house to help these three rats steal your goods. Call the city guard at once and don't let them escape!" Kochesh motioned to the servants, who stepped between Nahath and the trio.

"You liar!" Josiah shouted at Kochesh, who seized Josiah's harp from him and then the girls' instruments from them.

"Enough of that!" came the voice of Adaiah, who shoved Nahath out of his way and barged into the room ahead of Shammoth. The Levite knocked one servant bodily to the floor. Shammoth disarmed the other and struck him hard.

"Robbers!" Kochesh spat and snatched Josiah's sword from its sheath, then seized Hannah around the neck with his free arm. Stepping sideways, he planted a kick in Adaiah's stomach, doubling him over. The servant Adaiah had floored now rose and hurled himself on Adaiah in a rage. Kochesh brandished the sword menacingly, nearly choking Hannah, keeping Nahath and Shammoth at bay.

Rachel was the one he couldn't see, and Rachel was the one who surprised everybody by grabbing the back of the Philistine's hair and wrenching it downward. It was a foolish tactic against a man wielding a sword, but Kochesh by reflex released Hannah and backhanded Rachel with his freed hand. Shammoth seized the opportunity to lunge at Kochesh and engage him.

The girls darted across the room to Nahath. Josiah watched Shammoth and Kochesh cross swords rapidly. The blades flashed and clinked. Then another motion caught his eye and proved to be Casil, entering from the courtyard, armed with a loaded sling. He shot a hateful glance at Josiah and started whirling the sling, staring at the two fighting men. Josiah watched amazed as his former friend loosed a clumsy shot that hit Shammoth in the small of his back. The soldier fell to the floor and rolled away from Kochesh, who laughed.

Josiah was gripped by an instant rage. He flew at Casil and shoved him down with all his might. Casil, blindsided, fell and dropped his sling and two stones. Josiah swept them off the floor and loaded the sling without looking at Kochesh. Kochesh, flanked by both the household servants plus two more armed servants who had just arrived, was gloating at the Israelite men. "Get out of this good man's house and take your troublesome runts with you! Get out of this city, if you can, before I have your hands cut off for thievery!"

"Those instruments and that sword belong to the children," Adaiah growled.

"Liar!" Kochesh spat. "Now be gone before we slice you up ourselves!"

The harp and other instruments Kochesh had thrown into a far corner he now blocked from the Israelites. Josiah looked at Kochesh and began whirling the sling. "Kochesh, you're a liar and a thief," he said coldly. Kochesh and the Philistines turned to Josiah and immediately flinched at the sight of his twirling sling.

"Drop the stone, mighty man," Kochesh sneered. "You can hit but one of us. The others will hack you to pieces."

"There is only *one* of *you*," was the reply that took all the bluster out of Kochesh. Josiah spun the sling faster and faster. The Philistines scrambled backward in alarm. Josiah eyed his target and let fly the stone. It shot across the big room and struck the harp squarely, shattering it to fragments.

Kochesh was momentarily stunned, then began to curse Josiah loudly. But Josiah was already out the front door with his father and friends close behind.

Epilogue

Why do they have to be so cute and gentle? A mean, ugly animal would make it much easier. Josiah watched the old priest finish inspecting the small white lamb for imperfections, then looked up at the bronze doors of the palace of Jehovah, bright in the mid-morning sun. *How many times will I have to do this? How many sins will have me up here with a knife in my hand?* He inspected the clean, keen bronze blade.

"Josiah, I really will do it for you, if you like," his father said from behind.

"I wanted to be my own man, Dad. And here I am, doing a man's job." *We have to be men, Josiah.* Casil's admonition rang in his mind. Casil, who was still in Ashkelon.

The priest nodded to him. Josiah laid the knife on the edge of the massive altar and placed both hands on the lamb's woolly head. He pressed it, prayed briefly, and then shivered when the lamb licked his hand with its soft, wet tongue. Josiah collected himself. He took up the knife again.

Looking into its eyes, he thought, *So you die because I degraded the Word of Jehovah among the Philistines? Is it really that bad?* He looked again toward the palace doors, and sighed. *I've spent years learning that sacred Word and how to prophesy with music. I made it a light thing, a common thing, and used it to amuse those who hate Jehovah. I made Him like their despicable gods, and I knew better.* That was that; now either he obeyed or refused. It had been his own request to make this sin offering, though at that moment he wanted more than anything to offer only offerings of music for the rest of his life. But he would sin again, of course. And one day he, like his father, would even have a family to represent.

He clasped the back of the lamb's neck with his left hand. He then pressed the knife against its throat and held his breath. Willing his hand to act, he quickly cut and stepped back.

He still stood there as the priest collected the animal's blood and sprinkled it around the altar. Next, the priest took a large knife and divided the carcass. Finally, he placed all the pieces on the altar and set fire to the wood underneath.

Josiah watched flames devour what remained of the lamb he had just killed. He didn't move until his father's hand rested on his shoulder. "Let's go, my son. There are more people waiting to make sin offerings."

Notes to the Reader

The god Bull

One other god the Canaanites worshiped was the "father god." He was pictured as somewhat elderly and inactive—retired, perhaps—and often called by the general word for god, *El*. However, he was also commonly called Bull El, or "the god Bull." Idols of him appeared as calves or bulls. It may have been this god that the golden calf of Exodus 32 was based on.

The Philistines

Isaac encountered a people called Philistines in Genesis, a thousand years before the events of Solomon's day. However, these people were a different civilization than the later Philistines. Although they may have been from the same general location, the early Philistines did not share the culture of the later people and were probably not their ancestors.

Many different groups of people made up the great migration of the Sea Peoples, as the Egyptians collectively called them. These Sea Peoples appear to have come from the Aegean Sea region (Greece, Thrace, and western Asia Minor) during the time of the Judges in Israel. It is not known for certain why they migrated in such large numbers, but they were intent on establishing a new home by dominating Anatolia and Canaan.

They landed on the coastal plain of Canaan and built the cities of the Philistine Pentapolis ("five city"), a league of five cities with independent rulers. By controlling the fertile lowlands and keeping a monopoly on iron, which was just gaining widespread use, the Philistines sought to rule all of the land God had given Israel as the Promised Land.

Judges 10:6 first records that Israel sinned by serving "the gods of the Philistines" along with many other foreign gods. God allowed those same foreign nations, including the Philistines, to oppress Israel as punishment for their sin and as a way to bring

Israel to repentance. When Israel repented, God began to deliver them from the Philistine oppression.

Samson, the strong man, was raised up as a judge specifically to fight the Philistines. Despite repeatedly sinning and violating his consecration to God, Samson was used of God to inflict heavy damage on the Philistines. He killed more than a thousand Philistine men during his lifetime and three thousand more, many of high rank, at his death (Judges 16:23-31).

Samuel was the last judge and first prophet God raised up in Israel. He led Israel in a revival of faithfulness to Jehovah at a place called Mizpeh, then led them to a great victory over the Philistines at Eben-ezer (I Samuel 7). Later King Saul fought a seesaw war with them, winning when he obeyed Jehovah and losing when he was sinful. He was killed in his last great battle with the Philistines in Mount Gilboa.

David is well known for killing the giant Philistine champion Goliath in single combat. God honored David's faith and gave him a victory over the giant, and that event led to a victory over the whole Philistine army. Unfortunately, because King Saul, in rebellion against Jehovah, wanted to kill David, David had to flee Israel and seek shelter among the Philistines, his former enemy. David even offered once to help the Philistines fight Saul and Israel, but in God's providence the five Philistine lords refused his help; they feared he would betray them during the battle. After he became king of all twelve tribes of Israel, David defeated the Philistines and apparently broke their power permanently, because they did not trouble Israel again (II Samuel 8:1).

The five cities in the Pentapolis were Ashdod, Ashkelon, Ekron, Gaza, and Gath. They formed a close alliance with an advanced, organized society much like the Mycenaean (early Greek) civilization from which they originated. The inhabitants were accomplished as artists, architects, and soldiers. Though their original speech must have been quite different, they apparently adopted the language of southern Canaan since David, in his encounters with them, had no difficulty communicating. While it may not have been identical to the language of Israel, all Semitic languages were similar, and many would have been mutually intelligible. It is thus no surprise that Josiah and his friends are able to talk to the Philistines.

Clean and Unclean Animals

God told Noah to take seven of every clean animal and two of every unclean animal with him into the ark (Genesis 7:2). Nothing prior in Genesis tells which animals were clean and unclean. Although God may have revealed what He considered clean and unclean, it is possible that the distinction was just a societal standard. In other words, everyone just thought of certain animals as clean and dirty. Most societies do this, including our own. Modern Americans consider some animals appropriate for food and others not. For example, Americans eat plenty of pigs, cattle, chickens, fish, and shellfish, but on the whole they avoid dogs, cats, horses, snakes, and insects. Moreover, in America only the muscles of an animal are generally consumed; organs such as the lungs, liver, and kidneys are rejected. In other modern cultures, the muscles are repugnant; a civilized person eats only the organs.

God was not concerned with the animal itself but with what people thought of the animal. Some of these animals were to be used for sacrifice (Genesis 8:20). What would it have shown about Noah's view of God if he had offered animals he considered personally repulsive? It would have shown that he had little respect for God. On the other hand, if Noah offered animals he considered clean, the kind he himself would have eaten, he would have shown great respect for God by surrendering something of personal benefit.

The unclean animals were not necessarily loathsome just to be around. The law God gave to Israel made pigs unclean. Israelites probably did not keep pigs, since pigs have little value other than for food. But the law also made camels, donkeys, and horses unclean. Israelites used these animals for work but not for food or sacrifice. Josiah, consequently, is unfamiliar with pigs but thinks nothing of the camels walking around him. He would never eat one, but riding one is not a problem.

Other nations in the ancient Near East had ideas about clean and unclean animals that were similar to the laws God gave Israel. They generally sacrificed the same animals to their false gods—sheep, goats, and cattle—that Israel sacrificed to Jehovah. All were suitable for human food.

Review and Discussion

1. What incidents or circumstances occur that should have made Josiah more suspicious of Kochesh?

2. What are some significant differences between the worship of Jehovah and the worship described in Ashkelon?

3. Are there any reasons to believe that Josiah's conscience is troubling him about remaining in Ashkelon? If so, what are they?

4. Casil gives what reasons for accepting Kochesh's offer?

5. Do Kochesh and Abdod appear trustworthy or untrustworthy? Explain your answer.